SHIMBA
BIBLE STUDY SERIES

THE DIVINITY OF JESUS

IN THE BOOK OF DANIEL

Dr. Maxwell Shimba

SHIMBA
PUBLISHING

TABLE OF CONTENTS

INTRODUCTION

The Divine Revelation of Jesus Christ in the Book of Daniel

The Book of Daniel, an extraordinary compilation of prophetic visions and narratives, stands as a cornerstone of biblical prophecy. It holds a unique place in the Old Testament, bridging the gap between historical events and the divine revelations that foreshadow the coming of Jesus Christ. In this book, we will explore the profound lessons and divine nature of Jesus Christ as illustrated in the Book of Daniel, with a particular focus on Chapter 9, which vividly prophesies the coming of the Savior.

The Significance of Daniel

Daniel's life and ministry occurred during a tumultuous period in Israel's history. Taken captive as a young man to Babylon, Daniel's faithfulness to God amidst a pagan empire earned him a place of prominence and respect. His unwavering commitment to God provided him with unique visions and interpretations that revealed God's sovereign plan for humanity. The narratives of Daniel's courage and the apocalyptic visions he received are not just historical accounts but are imbued with deep theological significance.

Prophetic Visions and Messianic Hope

Central to the Book of Daniel are its apocalyptic visions, which include symbolic representations of empires and rulers. These visions extend beyond the immediate future of Israel and point to an ultimate resolution in the person of Jesus Christ. The prophecies contained in Daniel are crucial for understanding the messianic hope that pervades the Old Testament.

In Chapter 9, Daniel receives a vision of seventy weeks, which is a complex and highly debated prophecy. This prophecy outlines a timeline that culminates in the arrival of the Anointed One, the Messiah, who is to be "cut off" for the sake of many. This chapter is pivotal because it directly points to the coming of Jesus, His sacrificial death, and the establishment of a new covenant between God and His people.

Jesus Christ: The Fulfillment of Prophecy

The New Testament presents Jesus Christ as the fulfillment of the Old Testament prophecies. The Gospels often reference Daniel's visions, particularly the title "Son of Man" which Jesus frequently uses for Himself. This title, derived from Daniel 7:13-14, signifies the divine authority and eternal kingdom of the Messiah. Understanding these connections enriches our comprehension of Jesus' identity and mission.

Lessons from Jesus' Teachings

Jesus' teachings, as recorded in the Gospels, are imbued with wisdom, compassion, and authority. They address every aspect of human existence, offering guidance on how to live in alignment with God's will. By examining these teachings in light of Daniel's prophecies, we gain a deeper appreciation of their divine origin and purpose. The parables, the Beatitudes, and the numerous acts of healing and compassion reflect the fulfillment of God's promises revealed to Daniel.

The Coming Kingdom

Both Daniel and Jesus speak extensively about the Kingdom of God. Daniel's visions of the everlasting kingdom, ruled by the "Son of Man," are echoed in Jesus' proclamation of the Kingdom of Heaven. This kingdom is not of this world but is a spiritual reality that transforms the hearts and lives of believers. By aligning ourselves with the teachings of Jesus, we become part of this eternal kingdom, experiencing its transformative power in our daily lives.

Structure of This Book

This book is structured to guide you through the rich tapestry of Daniel's prophecies and Jesus' teachings. We will begin with an overview of Daniel's life and the historical context of his prophecies. Subsequent chapters will delve into specific visions, such as the fiery furnace, the dream of Nebuchadnezzar, and the seventy-week prophecy, drawing connections to Jesus' life and ministry.

We will also explore the core lessons from Jesus' teachings, examining their practical applications and spiritual significance. By doing so, we hope to illuminate the profound truths that both Daniel and Jesus imparted, offering you a comprehensive understanding of their message.

The Journey Ahead

As you embark on this journey through the Book of Daniel and the life of Jesus Christ, prepare to encounter divine wisdom and transformative insights. This exploration will not only deepen your faith but also provide you with a greater appreciation of the interconnectedness of God's Word. The revelations contained within these sacred texts are timeless, offering hope and guidance for believers across the ages.

May this book serve as a source of inspiration and enlightenment, drawing you closer to the heart of God and His divine plan as revealed through His Son, Jesus Christ.

DR. MAXWELL SHIMBA

THE PROPHETIC VISION OF DANIEL

Overview of the Book of Daniel

The Book of Daniel stands as a significant and multifaceted text within the Old Testament, notable for its blend of narrative history and apocalyptic prophecy. Its composition spans twelve chapters, divided into two distinct sections: the historical narratives (Chapters 1-6) and the apocalyptic visions (Chapters 7-12). This chapter provides an overview of Daniel, offering an expository study with comprehensive commentary, using Bible verses and an exhaustive Strong's Concordance to illuminate its profound messages.

Historical Context and Composition

The Book of Daniel is set during the Babylonian exile, a period when the Jewish people were taken captive by King Nebuchadnezzar of Babylon (Daniel 1:1-2). This exile serves as the backdrop for the events and visions described in the text. Daniel, the book's namesake, is a young nobleman taken into Babylonian service, whose faithfulness to God amidst a pagan empire becomes a central theme.

The book is traditionally attributed to Daniel himself, although modern scholarship offers varied perspectives on its authorship and dating. Regardless, its theological and prophetic insights remain timeless.

The Historical Narratives (Chapters 1-6)

Chapter 1: Daniel's Training in Babylon

Daniel 1 recounts the selection of Daniel and his friends—Hananiah, Mishael, and Azariah—for training in the Babylonian court. Despite the pressure to conform, they remain faithful to their dietary laws, resulting in God's favor (Daniel 1:8-16). Daniel 1:17 emphasizes God's gift to Daniel: "God gave them knowledge and skill in all learning and wisdom: and Daniel had understanding in all visions and dreams."

Chapter 2: Nebuchadnezzar's Dream

In Daniel 2, King Nebuchadnezzar's troubling dream of a colossal statue, which no Babylonian wise man can interpret, sets the stage for Daniel's divine insight. With God's revelation, Daniel interprets the dream, predicting a succession of empires and the ultimate establishment of God's everlasting kingdom (Daniel 2:31-45). This chapter introduces the theme of divine sovereignty over earthly kingdoms.

Chapter 3: The Fiery Furnace

Daniel 3 narrates the story of Shadrach, Meshach, and Abednego, who refuse to worship Nebuchadnezzar's golden image and are cast into a fiery furnace. Their miraculous preservation, with a fourth figure appearing in the flames (Daniel 3:25), signifies God's protective power and foreshadows the presence of Christ in trials.

Chapter 4: Nebuchadnezzar's Humbling

Nebuchadnezzar's second dream in Daniel 4, depicting a great tree cut down, symbolizes his impending madness and restoration. Daniel's interpretation and the fulfillment of this prophecy (Daniel 4:24-37) underscore God's ability to humble the proud and exalt the humble.

Chapter 5: Belshazzar's Feast

In Daniel 5, King Belshazzar's desecration of sacred temple vessels results in a mysterious handwriting on the wall. Daniel interprets the writing as a divine judgment against Belshazzar's arrogance, leading to the fall of Babylon that very night (Daniel 5:30).

Chapter 6: Daniel in the Lion's Den

Daniel 6 recounts Daniel's faithfulness during the reign of Darius the Mede. Despite a decree prohibiting prayer to any god but the king, Daniel continues his devotion to God, resulting in his being thrown into a lion's den. His miraculous deliverance (Daniel 6:22) highlights God's sovereignty and protection over His faithful servants.

The Apocalyptic Visions (Chapters 7-12)

Chapter 7: The Vision of the Four Beasts

Daniel 7 transitions to apocalyptic visions, beginning with four beasts representing successive empires. The vision culminates with the "Ancient of Days" and the "Son of Man" receiving eternal dominion (Daniel 7:13-14). This vision introduces the messianic figure of the Son of Man, a title Jesus frequently used for Himself.

Chapter 8: The Vision of the Ram and Goat

In Daniel 8, the vision of a ram and a goat symbolizes the Medo-Persian and Greek empires, respectively. The detailed prophecy of the rise and fall of these empires, including the emergence of a fierce king, underscores God's control over historical events (Daniel 8:20-25).

Chapter 9: The Seventy Weeks Prophecy

Daniel 9 features Daniel's prayer for his people and the angel Gabriel's response, revealing the seventy weeks prophecy. This prophecy, a timeline leading to the arrival of the Anointed One, predicts significant events including the

Messiah's death (Daniel 9:24-27). This chapter is pivotal for understanding the messianic timeline.

Chapter 10: The Heavenly Messenger

Daniel 10 presents a vision of a heavenly being who provides Daniel with insight into the spiritual battles influencing earthly events. This chapter sets the stage for the detailed prophecies in the following chapters (Daniel 10:13-14).

Chapter 11: The Kings of the South and North

Daniel 11 offers a detailed prophecy of future conflicts between the Ptolemaic and Seleucid empires, leading up to the time of the end. The accuracy of these predictions underscores the reliability of biblical prophecy (Daniel 11:2-35).

Chapter 12: The Time of the End

The final chapter, Daniel 12, provides a vision of the resurrection and final judgment. Daniel 12:2-3 speaks of the resurrection to everlasting life or contempt, highlighting the ultimate hope for the righteous and the fate of the wicked.

Theological Themes and Prophetic Significance

The Book of Daniel is rich in theological themes, including divine sovereignty, faithfulness in adversity, and the ultimate triumph of God's kingdom. Its apocalyptic visions provide a framework for understanding the unfolding of divine history and the coming of the Messiah.

Comprehensive Commentary and Strong's Concordance

A comprehensive study of Daniel involves examining the original Hebrew and Aramaic terms to fully grasp the text's meaning. Using Strong's Concordance, we can delve into key terms such as:

- "Visions" (Hebrew: חָזוֹן, Chazon, Strong's H2377): Refers to divine revelations given to Daniel (Daniel 7:1).

- "Kingdom" (Aramaic: מַלְכוּ, Malku, Strong's H4437): Denotes the rule and dominion of God (Daniel 2:44).

- "Son of Man" (Aramaic: בַּר אֱנָשׁ, Bar Enash, Strong's H1247): A title for the messianic figure seen in Daniel 7:13.

These terms and their usage within Daniel provide deeper insight into the text's prophetic messages.

Conclusion

The Book of Daniel offers a profound exploration of God's sovereignty, the faithfulness of His servants, and the ultimate fulfillment of His divine plan through Jesus Christ. This overview sets the stage for a detailed examination of Daniel's prophetic visions and their connections to the teachings of Jesus. By understanding the historical context, theological themes, and prophetic significance of Daniel, we gain a richer appreciation of its enduring relevance and divine wisdom.

Chapter 1: The Historical and Theological Contexts of the Book of Daniel

Historical Context

The historical context of the Book of Daniel is essential for understanding its narratives and prophecies. The events described span from the late 7th century to the early 6th century BCE, during the Babylonian exile of the Jewish people.

The Babylonian Exile

In 605 BCE, Nebuchadnezzar II, king of Babylon, defeated Pharaoh Necho II at the Battle of Carchemish, establishing Babylonian dominance over the Near East. This victory led to the first deportation of Jews to Babylon, including Daniel and his friends (Daniel 1:1-4). The Babylonian exile marks a significant period in Jewish history, characterized by the displacement and suffering of the Jewish people, but also by profound theological reflection and development.

Daniel in Babylon

Daniel, taken as a young nobleman, was trained in the language and literature of the Babylonians (Daniel 1:3-4). Despite his high position in the Babylonian court, Daniel remained steadfast in his faith, providing a powerful testimony to the God of Israel amidst a pagan empire.

The Persian Conquest

In 539 BCE, Babylon fell to the Persian Empire under Cyrus the Great. This transition of power is also reflected in Daniel, as Daniel continued to serve under Darius the Mede and Cyrus (Daniel 6:28). The Persian period brought new challenges and opportunities for the Jewish exiles, including the decree of Cyrus allowing the return to Jerusalem (Ezra 1:1-4).

Theological Context

The Book of Daniel is not just a historical document but a profound theological work. It addresses themes such as divine sovereignty, faithfulness, and eschatological hope.

Divine Sovereignty

A central theme in Daniel is the sovereignty of God over the affairs of nations and history. This is vividly depicted in Nebuchadnezzar's dream of the statue (Daniel 2) and the vision of the four beasts (Daniel 7), where God's kingdom ultimately triumphs over earthly empires. Daniel 2:44 declares, "And in the days of these kings shall the God of heaven set up a kingdom, which shall never be destroyed."

Faithfulness in Adversity

Daniel and his friends exemplify unwavering faithfulness to God despite immense pressure to conform. Their refusal to defile themselves with the king's food (Daniel 1), their deliverance from the fiery furnace (Daniel 3), and Daniel's survival in the lion's den (Daniel 6) demonstrate God's protection and favor towards those who remain loyal to Him.

Eschatological Hope

Daniel's visions provide a glimpse into the future, offering hope to the Jewish people. The prophecy of the seventy weeks (Daniel 9) and the vision of the resurrection (Daniel 12) point to the ultimate redemption and restoration of God's people. Daniel 12:2-3 speaks of the resurrection, "And many of them that sleep in the dust of the earth shall awake, some to everlasting life, and some to shame and everlasting contempt."

Expository Study and Strong's Concordance

An expository study of Daniel involves a careful analysis of the text, including its original language. Using Strong's Concordance, we can explore key Hebrew and Aramaic terms that deepen our understanding of the book's messages.

Key Terms

- "Dream" (Hebrew: חֲלוֹם, Chalom, Strong's H2472): Refers to the visions received by Nebuchadnezzar and Daniel. Dreams play a significant role in revealing God's plans (Daniel 2:1, 7:1).

- "Vision" (Hebrew: חָזוֹן, Chazon, Strong's H2377): Represents divine revelations given to Daniel (Daniel 8:1). These visions often contain symbolic imagery that requires interpretation.

- "Kingdom" (Aramaic: מַלְכוּ, Malku, Strong's H4437): Denotes the rule and dominion of God. The eternal kingdom of God is a recurring theme (Daniel 2:44, 7:27).

- "Son of Man" (Aramaic: בַּר אֱנָשׁ, Bar Enash, Strong's H1247): A title for the messianic figure in Daniel 7:13, later used by Jesus to refer to Himself, highlighting His divine authority and role.

Comprehensive Commentary

- Daniel 1:1-2: The opening verses set the historical stage, describing the conquest of Jerusalem by Nebuchadnezzar and the beginning of the exile. These events fulfill earlier prophecies of judgment against Judah (2 Kings 24:1-4).

- Daniel 2:31-45: Nebuchadnezzar's dream of a statue, composed of various materials, symbolizes successive empires. The stone that destroys the statue and becomes a great mountain represents God's eternal kingdom. This passage emphasizes the transient nature of human kingdoms compared to the everlasting dominion of God.

- Daniel 3:24-25: The deliverance of Shadrach, Meshach, and Abednego from the fiery furnace, with the appearance of a fourth figure "like the Son of God," prefigures Christ's presence and salvation. This account underscores God's power to save and His presence with His people in times of trial.

- Daniel 7:13-14: The vision of the Son of Man coming with the clouds of heaven, receiving dominion and glory, is a pivotal messianic prophecy. Jesus' frequent use of the title "Son of Man" in the Gospels (e.g., Matthew 26:64) directly connects to this vision, affirming His divine authority and eternal kingship.

- Daniel 9:24-27: The prophecy of seventy weeks outlines God's plan for Israel, culminating in the coming of the Anointed One. This passage is crucial for understanding the messianic timeline and the atoning work of Christ. The reference to the Anointed One being "cut off" points to Jesus' sacrificial death.

- Daniel 12:2-3: The promise of resurrection and eternal life for the righteous offers hope and assurance of God's ultimate justice. This eschatological vision aligns with

New Testament teachings on the resurrection (1 Corinthians 15:52-54) and eternal life.

Conclusion

The historical and theological contexts of the Book of Daniel provide a rich foundation for understanding its narratives and prophecies. The book's portrayal of divine sovereignty, faithfulness in adversity, and eschatological hope offers timeless lessons for believers. Through a detailed expository study and the use of Strong's Concordance, we can uncover the profound messages embedded in this prophetic text.

By examining the historical backdrop of the Babylonian exile and the theological themes that pervade the book, we gain a deeper appreciation for Daniel's role as a faithful servant and visionary prophet. As we continue our journey through the Book of Daniel, we will explore how these historical and theological contexts illuminate the lessons and divine nature of Jesus Christ.

Key Themes and Their Relevance to the Prophecy of the Messiah

The Book of Daniel is a rich tapestry of narrative history and apocalyptic prophecy, woven together to reveal profound theological themes. These themes not only highlight God's sovereignty and faithfulness but also point forward to the coming of the Messiah. This chapter will explore the key themes of the Book of Daniel and their relevance to the prophecy of the Messiah, providing a comprehensive understanding of how Daniel's visions and narratives foreshadow the life and mission of Jesus Christ.

Divine Sovereignty

One of the most prominent themes in the Book of Daniel is the sovereignty of God over human history. This theme is evident in the dreams and visions that depict the rise and fall of empires, demonstrating that God's kingdom ultimately prevails.

Nebuchadnezzar's Dream (Daniel 2)

In Daniel 2, Nebuchadnezzar's dream of a great statue composed of various materials—gold, silver, bronze, iron, and clay—represents successive kingdoms. The interpretation, given by Daniel, reveals that these kingdoms will be replaced by an eternal kingdom established by God (Daniel 2:44). This prophecy underscores God's control over earthly rulers and the transient nature of human power.

Relevance to the Messiah: The eternal kingdom that crushes all others is a direct reference to the messianic kingdom. Jesus Christ, the Messiah, inaugurates this kingdom, which transcends all earthly domains. In the New Testament,

Jesus speaks of the Kingdom of God (Mark 1:15), fulfilling the vision of a divine kingdom prophesied in Daniel.

The Vision of the Four Beasts (Daniel 7)

Daniel's vision of the four beasts coming out of the sea (Daniel 7:3-8) represents four empires. The fourth beast is particularly terrifying, with ten horns and a little horn that speaks arrogantly. The vision culminates in the appearance of the "Ancient of Days" and the "Son of Man," who is given dominion and an everlasting kingdom (Daniel 7:13-14).

Relevance to the Messiah: The "Son of Man" in Daniel's vision is a messianic figure, a title Jesus frequently used for Himself (Matthew 26:64). This vision portrays the ultimate authority and eternal reign of the Messiah, affirming Jesus' divine identity and His role in God's redemptive plan.

Faithfulness and Obedience

The theme of faithfulness and obedience to God is illustrated through the lives of Daniel and his friends, who remain steadfast in their devotion despite facing severe trials.

The Fiery Furnace (Daniel 3)

Shadrach, Meshach, and Abednego refuse to worship Nebuchadnezzar's golden image and are thrown into a fiery furnace. Their miraculous deliverance by a divine figure (Daniel 3:24-25) demonstrates God's protection and the power of unwavering faith.

Relevance to the Messiah: This story prefigures the saving power of Christ. Just as the three men are saved from physical death, Jesus saves humanity from spiritual death. The fourth figure in the furnace, often seen as a pre-incarnate appearance of Christ, signifies His presence with and deliverance of His people.

Daniel in the Lion's Den (Daniel 6)

Daniel's refusal to cease praying to God, despite the decree of King Darius, leads to his being thrown into a lion's den. God shuts the mouths of the lions, protecting Daniel and vindicating his faithfulness (Daniel 6:22-23).

Relevance to the Messiah: Daniel's deliverance from the lions parallels Jesus' resurrection. Just as Daniel emerges unscathed from the den, Jesus conquers death, emerging victorious from the grave. Both stories emphasize the power of faith and God's ability to deliver and vindicate His faithful servants.

Apocalyptic Visions and Eschatological Hope

Daniel's apocalyptic visions provide a glimpse into the future, offering hope for the ultimate triumph of God's kingdom and the redemption of His people.

The Seventy Weeks Prophecy (Daniel 9)

In Daniel 9, the prophecy of seventy weeks outlines a timeline leading to the arrival of the Anointed One. This prophecy predicts significant events, including the coming of the Messiah, His sacrificial death, and the establishment of a new covenant (Daniel 9:24-27).

Relevance to the Messiah: The seventy-week prophecy is crucial for understanding the messianic timeline. The "Anointed One" being "cut off" refers to Jesus' crucifixion. This prophecy highlights Jesus' role as the Messiah who brings an end to sin and ushers in everlasting righteousness.

The Vision of the Resurrection (Daniel 12)

Daniel 12 presents a vision of the end times, including the resurrection of the dead. Daniel 12:2-3 speaks of a resurrection to either everlasting life or shame and contempt, emphasizing the final judgment and the hope of eternal life for the righteous.

Relevance to the Messiah: This vision aligns with New Testament teachings on the resurrection and eternal life through Christ (John 5:28-29). Jesus' resurrection is the firstfruits of this promise, offering believers the hope of eternal life and affirming the ultimate victory over death.

The Messianic Kingdom

Daniel's visions consistently point to a future messianic kingdom characterized by justice, peace, and eternal dominion.

The Stone That Becomes a Mountain (Daniel 2)

The stone that destroys the statue and becomes a great mountain represents God's kingdom, which will endure forever (Daniel 2:34-35, 44-45).

Relevance to the Messiah: This imagery is fulfilled in Christ, whose kingdom is not of this world but eternal and unshakeable (Hebrews 12:28). Jesus' teachings on the Kingdom of God reflect this vision, emphasizing a spiritual kingdom that transforms lives and will be fully realized in His second coming.

The Everlasting Kingdom (Daniel 7)

The "Son of Man" is given dominion, glory, and a kingdom that all peoples, nations, and languages should serve Him (Daniel 7:14). His dominion is everlasting and His kingdom will not be destroyed.

Relevance to the Messiah: Jesus' use of the title "Son of Man" signifies His fulfillment of this prophecy. His kingdom is characterized by divine authority, eternal duration, and universal reach, affirming His messianic role and the ultimate realization of God's plan for redemption and restoration.

The key themes in the Book of Daniel—divine sovereignty, faithfulness and obedience, apocalyptic visions, and the messianic kingdom—are deeply interwoven with the prophecy of the Messiah. Through these themes, Daniel provides a prophetic foundation that points forward to Jesus Christ, affirming His divine identity, His redemptive mission, and the ultimate establishment of His eternal kingdom. As we continue to explore the Book of Daniel, we will uncover the rich tapestry of prophetic messages that reveal the profound truths about the Messiah and His transformative impact on history and humanity.

CHAPTER 02

JESUS IN THE FIERY FURNACE

The story of Shadrach, Meshach, and Abednego in the fiery furnace is one of the most dramatic and inspiring narratives in the Book of Daniel. This account, found in Daniel 3, not only illustrates the unwavering faith of these three young men but also provides a powerful foreshadowing of the presence and saving power of Jesus Christ. In this chapter, we will delve deeply into the story, exploring its historical context, theological significance, and the profound lessons it offers for believers today.

Historical Context

The events of Daniel 3 take place during the reign of King Nebuchadnezzar of Babylon, who ruled from 605 to 562 BCE. After successfully conquering Jerusalem and deporting many of its inhabitants, Nebuchadnezzar sought to unify his diverse empire under a common religion and culture. One method he employed was the erection of a colossal golden image, demanding that all subjects worship it.

The Golden Image and the Decree

The chapter begins with Nebuchadnezzar constructing a golden image, which he set up on the plain of Dura in the province of Babylon (Daniel 3:1). This image, likely representing the king or a deity, was intended to be a focal point of loyalty and worship for the empire. Nebuchadnezzar summoned all the officials of his kingdom to the dedication of the image, issuing a decree that at the sound of musical instruments, everyone must fall down and worship the golden image (Daniel 3:2-5). Those who refused would be thrown into a blazing furnace (Daniel 3:6).

The Defiance of Shadrach, Meshach, and Abednego

Shadrach, Meshach, and Abednego, three Jewish officials appointed by Nebuchadnezzar himself (Daniel 1:7, 2:49), refused to obey the king's decree. Their refusal was reported to Nebuchadnezzar by certain Chaldeans, who were likely motivated by jealousy and a desire to eliminate these favored Jewish exiles (Daniel 3:8-12).

When brought before the king, Nebuchadnezzar gave them another chance to comply, warning them of the consequences and questioning, "Who is that God that shall deliver you out of my hands?" (Daniel 3:15). Their response is a profound testament to their faith:

"O Nebuchadnezzar, we are not careful to answer thee in this matter. If it be so, our God whom we serve is able to deliver us from the burning fiery furnace, and he will deliver us out of thine hand, O king. But if not, be it known unto thee, O king, that we will not serve thy gods, nor worship the golden image which thou hast set up" (Daniel 3:16-18).

The Fiery Furnace

Enraged by their defiance, Nebuchadnezzar ordered the furnace to be heated seven times hotter than usual and commanded his strongest soldiers to bind Shadrach, Meshach, and Abednego and cast them into the fire (Daniel 3:19-20). The furnace was so hot that the flames killed the soldiers who threw them in (Daniel 3:22).

The Divine Deliverance

As Nebuchadnezzar watched, expecting to see the men consumed by the flames, he was astonished to see four figures walking unharmed in the fire. The fourth figure, he noted, looked "like the Son of God" (Daniel 3:25). Nebuchadnezzar called them out of the furnace, and to the amazement of all, Shadrach, Meshach, and Abednego emerged unscathed, without even the smell of fire on their clothes (Daniel 3:26-27).

Recognizing the miracle, Nebuchadnezzar praised the God of Shadrach, Meshach, and Abednego, declaring, "Blessed be the God of Shadrach, Meshach, and Abednego, who hath sent his angel, and delivered the servants that trusted in him" (Daniel 3:28). He issued a decree that no one in the kingdom should speak against their God, "because there is no other God that can deliver after this sort" (Daniel 3:29). He then promoted Shadrach, Meshach, and Abednego in the province of Babylon (Daniel 3:30).

Theological Significance

The story of Shadrach, Meshach, and Abednego is rich in theological significance. It highlights several key themes that resonate throughout the Bible and are particularly relevant to the prophecy of the Messiah.

Faith and Obedience

The unwavering faith of Shadrach, Meshach, and Abednego in the face of death exemplifies true obedience to God. Their declaration, "But if not," acknowledges God's sovereignty and their willingness to remain faithful regardless of the outcome. This echoes the sentiments found in Hebrews 11, the "Faith Hall of Fame," where numerous figures are commended for their faith.

Divine Presence and Deliverance

The presence of the fourth figure in the furnace, identified by Nebuchadnezzar as "like the Son of God," is a powerful manifestation of divine presence and deliverance. This prefigures the incarnation of Jesus Christ, who is Emmanuel, "God with us" (Matthew 1:23). Just as Christ walked with Shadrach, Meshach, and Abednego in the furnace, He promises to be with His followers in their trials (John 16:33).

God's Sovereignty Over Earthly Powers

Nebuchadnezzar's recognition of God's power underscores the theme of divine sovereignty. Despite his absolute authority as a king, he acknowledges that the God of Israel is supreme. This aligns with the broader message of Daniel, where earthly kingdoms rise and fall, but God's kingdom endures forever (Daniel 2:44).

Lessons for Believers Today

The story of Shadrach, Meshach, and Abednego offers timeless lessons for believers today. It encourages unwavering faith in the face of adversity, trust in God's deliverance, and a recognition of His sovereignty over all aspects of life.

Faith in Adversity

Believers are called to stand firm in their faith, even when facing persecution or trials. The courage of Shadrach,

Meshach, and Abednego serves as a powerful example of how to remain steadfast in the face of opposition, trusting that God is with them.

Divine Deliverance

The miraculous deliverance from the fiery furnace reminds believers of God's power to save. While not all trials may result in such dramatic rescues, God's presence and support are assured. This story encourages believers to trust in God's timing and methods of deliverance.

Witness to Others

Nebuchadnezzar's transformation from a skeptic to a believer in the God of Israel demonstrates the impact of faithful witness. The faithfulness of Shadrach, Meshach, and Abednego not only saved their lives but also led to the proclamation of God's power throughout the Babylonian Empire. Believers today are called to be witnesses to God's power and love, impacting those around them through their faith and actions.

The story of Shadrach, Meshach, and Abednego in the fiery furnace is a testament to the power of faith, the presence of God in times of trial, and the ultimate sovereignty of God over all earthly powers. It prefigures the saving work of Jesus Christ, who walks with His followers through their own fires and delivers them from the ultimate furnace of sin and death.

As we reflect on this narrative, may it inspire us to remain steadfast in our faith, trust in God's deliverance, and boldly witness to His power and sovereignty. The story of these three young men, their courage, and their miraculous rescue continues to resonate as a powerful testimony of God's unchanging faithfulness and love.

The Fourth Figure in the Fire: A Prefiguration of Christ

The appearance of the fourth figure in the fiery furnace, described as "like the Son of God" (Daniel 3:25), is one of the most enigmatic and powerful moments in the Book of Daniel. This mysterious figure, who saves Shadrach, Meshach, and Abednego from certain death, has been traditionally interpreted by many Christians as a prefiguration of Christ. In this chapter, we will explore the identity and significance of this fourth figure, using Bible verses, expository study, and exhaustive Strong's Concordance to provide a comprehensive commentary on how this event foreshadows the person and work of Jesus Christ.

The Appearance of the Fourth Figure

The context of this appearance is crucial. Shadrach, Meshach, and Abednego, refusing to worship Nebuchadnezzar's golden image, are thrown into a furnace heated seven times hotter than usual (Daniel 3:19-20). As the king watches, he is astonished to see not three, but four men walking unbound and unharmed in the fire:

"Then Nebuchadnezzar the king was astonished, and rose up in haste, and spake, and said unto his counselors, Did not we cast three men bound into the midst of the fire? They answered and said unto the king, True, O king. He answered and said, Lo, I see four men loose, walking in the midst of the fire, and they have no hurt; and the form of the fourth is like the Son of God" (Daniel 3:24-25, KJV).

Expository Analysis and Strong's Concordance

To understand the significance of the fourth figure, we need to analyze the key terms and their usage in the original Aramaic text, as well as explore how this event fits into the broader biblical narrative.

"Son of God" (Aramaic: בַּר אֱלָהִין, bar 'elahin)

The phrase "Son of God" used by Nebuchadnezzar is translated from the Aramaic בַּר אֱלָהִין (bar 'elahin), which can mean "a son of the gods" or "divine being." This phrase indicates a recognition of the figure's divine or supernatural nature, even if Nebuchadnezzar, a polytheist, did not fully understand the identity of the fourth figure.

Strong's Concordance:

- Bar (בַּר): Strong's H1247, meaning "son."

- 'Elahin (אֱלָהִין): Strong's H426, a plural form of the word for "God" or "gods."

This linguistic analysis shows that Nebuchadnezzar recognized the figure as divine, which sets the stage for understanding this figure as a pre-incarnate appearance of Christ, known as a Christophany.

Christophany: Pre-incarnate Appearances of Christ

A Christophany is an appearance of the pre-incarnate Christ in the Old Testament. Such appearances reveal Christ's involvement in God's plan of redemption throughout history, even before His incarnation.

Other Examples of Christophanies

- The Angel of the Lord: Many Old Testament appearances of "the Angel of the Lord" are considered Christophanies. For example, the Angel of the Lord appears to Hagar (Genesis 16:7-13), Abraham (Genesis 22:11-18), Moses (Exodus 3:2-6), and Gideon (Judges 6:11-24). In these instances, the Angel speaks with divine authority and is often identified as God Himself.

- The Commander of the Lord's Army: In Joshua 5:13-15, Joshua encounters a divine warrior who identifies Himself as the Commander of the Lord's Army, a figure often interpreted as the pre-incarnate Christ.

These appearances, like the fourth figure in the fiery furnace, demonstrate Christ's active presence and intervention in the lives of His people before His incarnation.

The Fourth Figure in the Furnace

The fourth figure in the furnace shares several characteristics with other Christophanies:

- Divine Appearance: Nebuchadnezzar immediately recognizes the figure's divine nature, describing Him as "like the Son of God" (Daniel 3:25).

- Deliverance and Protection: The figure delivers Shadrach, Meshach, and Abednego from the flames, paralleling the protective and salvific roles Christ plays throughout the Bible.

- Presence with the Faithful: The fourth figure's presence in the fire symbolizes Christ's promise to be with His followers in times of trial and suffering, as affirmed in the New Testament (Matthew 28:20, John 16:33).

Theological Significance

The appearance of the fourth figure has profound theological implications, particularly when viewed through the lens of Christology.

Christ's Presence in Suffering

The fourth figure's presence in the furnace highlights a key aspect of Christ's ministry: His presence with His people in their suffering. This prefigures Jesus' earthly ministry, where He frequently associated with and comforted the afflicted (Matthew 11:28-30, John 14:27).

Biblical References:

- Isaiah 43:2: "When thou passest through the waters, I will be with thee; and through the rivers, they shall not overflow thee: when thou walkest through the fire, thou shalt not be burned; neither shall the flame kindle upon thee." This verse promises God's presence in times of trouble, fulfilled by Christ's presence in the fiery furnace.

- Hebrews 13:5: "I will never leave thee, nor forsake thee." This assurance of God's continual presence is embodied in Christ's role as Emmanuel, "God with us" (Matthew 1:23).

Divine Deliverance

The deliverance of Shadrach, Meshach, and Abednego from the furnace prefigures the ultimate deliverance offered by Christ through His death and resurrection. Just as the fourth figure saved them from physical death, Jesus saves humanity from spiritual death.

Biblical References:

- John 3:16: "For God so loved the world, that he gave his only begotten Son, that whosoever believeth in him should not perish, but have everlasting life."

- Romans 8:38-39: Paul's affirmation that nothing can separate believers from the love of God in Christ Jesus echoes the inseparable bond demonstrated by the fourth figure's presence in the furnace.

Sovereignty Over Earthly Powers

Nebuchadnezzar's recognition of the fourth figure's divinity and subsequent decree glorifying God (Daniel 3:28-29) underscores the theme of divine sovereignty. Christ's ultimate authority over earthly powers is a central theme in the New Testament.

Biblical References:

- Philippians 2:9-11: "Wherefore God also hath highly exalted him, and given him a name which is above every name: That at the name of Jesus every knee should bow... and that every tongue should confess that Jesus Christ is Lord, to the glory of God the Father."

- Revelation 1:5: Jesus is described as "the ruler of the kings of the earth," affirming His supreme authority.

Comprehensive Commentary

A deeper understanding of the fourth figure can be gained through comprehensive commentary and cross-referencing other biblical passages.

Daniel 3:24-25:

- The astonishment of Nebuchadnezzar and his declaration of seeing four men "loose, walking in the midst of the fire" emphasizes the miraculous nature of their deliverance.

- Nebuchadnezzar's description of the fourth figure as "like the Son of God" suggests an encounter with a divine being, consistent with the concept of a Christophany.

Isaiah 43:2:

- This promise of divine protection resonates with the experience of Shadrach, Meshach, and Abednego, highlighting God's faithfulness in fulfilling His promises.

Matthew 28:20:

- Jesus' assurance, "I am with you always," is prefigured by the fourth figure's presence in the furnace, illustrating the continuity of God's promise of presence from the Old Testament to the New Testament.

John 3:16:

- The deliverance from physical death in the furnace prefigures the spiritual deliverance through Jesus' sacrifice, emphasizing the continuity of God's redemptive plan.

Revelation 1:5:

- Christ's authority over earthly powers, acknowledged by Nebuchadnezzar, is fully realized in the New Testament portrayal of Jesus as the sovereign ruler.

The appearance of the fourth figure in the fiery furnace is a profound prefiguration of Christ. This event not only underscores the themes of divine presence, deliverance, and sovereignty but also provides a vivid illustration of Christ's role in God's redemptive plan. By examining this Christophany, we gain deeper insights into the nature of Christ and His enduring presence with His people.

As we reflect on the story of Shadrach, Meshach, and Abednego, may we be inspired by their unwavering faith and encouraged by the assurance of Christ's presence in our own trials. The fourth figure in the fire stands as a powerful testament to the saving power and eternal presence of Jesus Christ, our Savior, and Redeemer.

Lessons of Faith, Deliverance, and Divine Presence

The story of Shadrach, Meshach, and Abednego in the fiery furnace is a powerful testament to faith, divine deliverance, and the assurance of God's presence. This narrative, found in Daniel 3, offers timeless lessons that resonate deeply with believers today. In this chapter, we will explore these lessons in detail, examining how the faith of these three men, their miraculous deliverance, and the divine presence in the furnace serve as profound spiritual truths and encouragements for contemporary faith journeys.

The Faith of Shadrach, Meshach, and Abednego

The unwavering faith of Shadrach, Meshach, and Abednego is central to the narrative in Daniel 3. Their refusal to worship Nebuchadnezzar's golden image, despite the threat of death, exemplifies a steadfast commitment to God.

Absolute Trust in God

When confronted with the ultimatum to worship the image or face the fiery furnace, Shadrach, Meshach, and Abednego respond with unwavering confidence in God's ability to save them:

"O Nebuchadnezzar, we are not careful to answer thee in this matter. If it be so, our God whom we serve is able to deliver us from the burning fiery furnace, and he will deliver us out of thine hand, O king" (Daniel 3:16-17, KJV).

Lessons for Believers:

- Unyielding Faith: Their response teaches us to maintain our faith in God, even when facing seemingly insurmountable challenges. This level of trust requires a deep, personal relationship with God, built through prayer, study, and obedience.

- Confidence in God's Power: Their declaration of God's ability to deliver them reflects a profound understanding of His omnipotence. Believers are encouraged to trust in God's power and sovereignty over all circumstances.

Faith Despite Uncertainty

The trio's faith is further highlighted by their acceptance of God's will, even if it means death:

"But if not, be it known unto thee, O king, that we will not serve thy gods, nor worship the golden image which thou hast set up" (Daniel 3:18, KJV).

Lessons for Believers:

- Submission to God's Will: True faith includes submission to God's will, even when it does not align with our desires. Shadrach, Meshach, and Abednego's acceptance of potential martyrdom exemplifies a mature faith that trusts God's wisdom and plan.

- Faith Without Guarantees: Their stance teaches us that faith does not depend on guaranteed outcomes. Believers are called to trust in God's goodness and sovereignty, regardless of the immediate results.

Divine Deliverance

The miraculous deliverance of Shadrach, Meshach, and Abednego from the fiery furnace is a powerful demonstration of God's saving power.

God's Intervention

Nebuchadnezzar's astonishment at seeing four men walking unharmed in the fire underscores the miraculous nature of their deliverance:

"Then Nebuchadnezzar the king was astonished, and rose up in haste, and spake, and said unto his counselors, Did not we cast three men bound into the midst of the fire? They answered and said unto the king, True, O king. He answered and said, Lo, I see four men loose, walking in the midst of the fire, and they have no hurt; and the form of the fourth is like the Son of God" (Daniel 3:24-25, KJV).

Lessons for Believers:

- Miraculous Deliverance: The deliverance of Shadrach, Meshach, and Abednego serves as a reminder of God's ability to intervene miraculously in our lives. While not every trial results in such dramatic rescue, believers can trust that God is able to save and will act according to His will and purpose.

- Witness to God's Power: Their deliverance became a powerful testimony to Nebuchadnezzar and the Babylonian Empire, demonstrating God's supremacy over human authority and false gods. Believers are encouraged to view their trials as opportunities to witness God's power and faithfulness.

Preservation in Trials

The fact that Shadrach, Meshach, and Abednego emerge from the furnace without even the smell of fire on them highlights God's complete preservation:

"And the princes, governors, and captains, and the king's counselors, being gathered together, saw these men, upon whose bodies the fire had no power, nor was a hair of their head singed, neither were their coats changed, nor the smell of fire had passed on them" (Daniel 3:27, KJV).

Lessons for Believers:

- Total Protection: God's preservation of Shadrach, Meshach, and Abednego teaches us that His protection is complete. Even when we walk through life's fires, we can trust in God's ability to protect and preserve us.

- Endurance Through Faith: Their endurance through the furnace serves as an encouragement for believers to remain steadfast in their faith, knowing that God is with them in their trials and will bring them through.

Divine Presence

The presence of the fourth figure in the furnace is a powerful manifestation of God's presence with His people in times of trial.

The Fourth Figure

Nebuchadnezzar's recognition of the divine nature of the fourth figure, described as "like the Son of God," points to the pre-incarnate Christ's presence with His faithful servants:

"He answered and said, Lo, I see four men loose, walking in the midst of the fire, and they have no hurt; and the form of the fourth is like the Son of God" (Daniel 3:25, KJV).

Lessons for Believers:

- Christ's Presence in Suffering: The fourth figure represents Christ's presence with His followers in their suffering. Believers can find comfort in knowing that Jesus is with them in their trials, providing strength and assurance.

- Immanuel – God With Us: This event prefigures the New Testament revelation of Jesus as Immanuel, "God with us" (Matthew 1:23). The promise of God's presence is a recurring theme throughout the Bible, assuring believers of His constant companionship and support.

Assurance of Divine Presence

The story of Shadrach, Meshach, and Abednego assures believers of God's unchanging promise to be with them in all circumstances:

"When thou passest through the waters, I will be with thee; and through the rivers, they shall not overflow thee: when thou walkest through the fire, thou shalt not be burned; neither shall the flame kindle upon thee" (Isaiah 43:2, KJV).

Lessons for Believers:

- God's Faithfulness: God's promise to be with His people is a consistent theme throughout Scripture. Believers are encouraged to trust in God's faithfulness and presence, especially in times of trial.

- Enduring Faith: The presence of God with Shadrach, Meshach, and Abednego strengthens believers' faith, reminding them that they are never alone. This assurance helps them endure and overcome life's challenges with confidence.

The story of Shadrach, Meshach, and Abednego in the fiery furnace offers profound lessons on faith, deliverance, and divine presence. Their unwavering faith in the face of death, their miraculous deliverance, and the assurance of God's presence serve as powerful examples for believers today.

Through this narrative, we learn the importance of maintaining unyielding faith in God, trusting in His power and sovereignty, and submitting to His will, even in the face of uncertainty. The miraculous deliverance of Shadrach, Meshach, and Abednego reminds us of God's ability to save and His complete protection in trials. Finally, the presence of the fourth figure in the furnace assures us of Christ's presence with us in our suffering, providing comfort, strength, and assurance.

As we reflect on these lessons, may we be inspired to deepen our faith, trust in God's deliverance, and find peace in the assurance of His constant presence? The story of Shadrach, Meshach, and Abednego continues to resonate as a powerful testament to the faithfulness and love of God, encouraging believers to stand firm and trust in Him through all of life's challenges.

With their hearts set on the elusive promise of gold, John and Emily bid farewell to the comfort of their familiar lives. Their wagon, laden with supplies, creaked under the weight of their dreams as it rolled westward, leaving behind the only world they had ever known.

CHAPTER 03

THE DREAM OF NEBUCHADNEZZAR

Nebuchadnezzar's dream of the statue in Daniel 2 is one of the most significant prophetic visions in the Old Testament. This dream not only reveals the future succession of world empires but also underscores the sovereignty of God and His ultimate plan for an everlasting kingdom. In this chapter, we will examine Nebuchadnezzar's dream in detail, using Bible verses, expository study, and exhaustive Strong's Concordance to provide comprehensive commentary and insights.

The Dream and Its Context

The events of Daniel 2 occur in the second year of Nebuchadnezzar's reign. The king, troubled by a disturbing dream, demands its interpretation from his wise men.

However, he insists they first reveal the dream itself, an impossible task that leads to a crisis.

Nebuchadnezzar's Demand

Nebuchadnezzar's demand highlights his mistrust of the wise men and his desire for a genuine interpretation:

"And in the second year of the reign of Nebuchadnezzar, Nebuchadnezzar dreamed dreams, wherewith his spirit was troubled, and his sleep brake from him. Then the king commanded to call the magicians, and the astrologers, and the sorcerers, and the Chaldeans, for to shew the king his dreams. So they came and stood before the king. And the king said unto them, I have dreamed a dream, and my spirit was troubled to know the dream" (Daniel 2:1-3, KJV).

Lessons for Believers:

- Seeking Divine Wisdom: The king's demand for both the dream and its interpretation emphasizes the need for divine wisdom. This sets the stage for Daniel to demonstrate that true wisdom and revelation come from God.

The Failure of the Wise Men

The inability of the wise men to reveal the dream underscores their limitations and the uniqueness of God's revelation through Daniel:

"The Chaldeans answered before the king, and said, There is not a man upon the earth that can shew the king's matter: therefore there is no king, lord, nor ruler, that asked such things at any magician, or astrologer, or Chaldean. And it is a rare thing that the king requireth and there is none other that can shew it before the king, except the gods, whose dwelling is not with flesh" (Daniel 2:10-11, KJV).

Lessons for Believers:

- Human Limitations: The wise men's admission highlights human limitations and the necessity of seeking God's guidance and revelation in times of uncertainty.

Daniel's Intervention

Faced with the threat of death for all the wise men, Daniel seeks God's mercy and receives the revelation of the dream and its interpretation:

"Then Daniel went in, and desired of the king that he would give him time, and that he would shew the king the interpretation. Then Daniel went to his house and made the thing known to Hananiah, Mishael, and Azariah, his companions: That they would desire mercies of the God of heaven concerning this secret; that Daniel and his fellows should not perish with the rest of the wise men of Babylon. Then was the secret revealed unto Daniel in a night vision.

Then Daniel blessed the God of heaven" (Daniel 2:16-19, KJV).

Lessons for Believers:

- The Power of Prayer: Daniel's immediate response is to seek God's mercy through prayer, emphasizing the power of collective prayer and dependence on God in times of crisis.

- Divine Revelation: God's revelation to Daniel highlights His faithfulness in answering the prayers of His people and providing wisdom and guidance.

The Dream Revealed and Interpreted

Daniel's recounting of the dream and its interpretation reveals a prophetic timeline of world empires and the establishment of God's eternal kingdom.

The Dream Described

Daniel describes Nebuchadnezzar's dream, detailing a great statue composed of various materials:

"Thou, O king, sawest, and behold a great image. This great image, whose brightness was excellent, stood before thee; and the form thereof was terrible. This image's head was of fine gold, his breast and his arms of silver, his belly and his thighs of brass, His legs of iron, his feet part of iron and part of clay. Thou sawest till that a stone was cut out without hands, which smote the image upon his feet that were of iron and clay, and brake them to pieces" (Daniel 2:31-34, KJV).

Lessons for Believers:

- Symbolism of the Statue: The different materials of the statue symbolize successive world empires, illustrating the transient nature of human kingdoms in contrast to God's eternal kingdom.

The Interpretation

Daniel's interpretation provides a detailed explanation of the dream's symbolism and its prophetic significance:

"This is the dream; and we will tell the interpretation thereof before the king. Thou, O king, art a king of kings: for the God of heaven hath given thee a kingdom, power, and strength, and glory. And wheresoever the children of men dwell, the beasts of the field and the fowls of the heaven hath he given into thine hand, and hath made thee ruler over them all. Thou art this head of gold. And after thee shall arise another kingdom inferior to thee, and another third kingdom of brass, which shall bear rule over all the earth. And the fourth kingdom shall be strong as iron: forasmuch as iron breaketh in pieces and subdueth all things: and as iron that breaketh all these, shall it break in pieces and bruise. And whereas thou sawest the feet and toes, part of potters' clay, and part of iron, the kingdom shall be divided; but there shall be in it of the strength of the iron, forasmuch as thou sawest the iron mixed with miry clay. And as the toes of the feet were part of iron, and part of clay, so the kingdom shall be partly strong, and partly broken. And whereas thou sawest iron mixed with miry clay, they shall mingle themselves with the seed of men: but they shall not cleave one to another, even as iron is not mixed with clay" (Daniel 2:36-43, KJV).

Lessons for Believers:

- God's Sovereignty Over History: The detailed succession of empires illustrates God's sovereignty over human history, demonstrating that all earthly kingdoms are subject to His ultimate authority.

The Stone and the Eternal Kingdom

The climax of the dream is the stone that destroys the statue and becomes a great mountain, representing God's eternal kingdom:

"And in the days of these kings shall the God of heaven set up a kingdom, which shall never be destroyed: and the kingdom shall not be left to other people, but it shall break in pieces and consume all these kingdoms, and it shall stand for ever. Forasmuch as thou sawest that the stone was cut out of the mountain without hands, and that it brake in pieces the iron, the brass, the clay, the silver, and the gold; the great God hath made known to the king what shall come to pass hereafter: and the dream is certain, and the interpretation thereof sure" (Daniel 2:44-45, KJV).

Lessons for Believers:

- The Messiah and the Kingdom of God: The stone "cut out without hands" symbolizes the divine origin of the Messiah and His kingdom. This eternal kingdom, established by Christ, will ultimately prevail over all earthly powers.

Expository Analysis and Strong's Concordance

Using Strong's Concordance, we can gain deeper insights into the key terms and concepts in this prophetic vision.

Key Terms

- Image (צֶלֶם, tselem, Strong's H6755): The term for the statue seen in Nebuchadnezzar's dream, symbolizing the kingdoms of the world.

- Kingdom (מַלְכוּ, malku, Strong's H4437): Refers to the various empires represented by the different parts of the statue and the ultimate kingdom of God.

- Stone (אֶבֶן, eben, Strong's H68): Represents the Messiah and the kingdom of God, "cut out without hands," indicating divine origin.

Comprehensive Commentary
Daniel 2:31-34:

- The statue's head of gold represents the Babylonian Empire under Nebuchadnezzar. The chest and arms of silver symbolize the Medo-Persian Empire, the belly and thighs of bronze represent the Greek Empire, and the legs of iron with feet partly of iron and clay depict the Roman Empire and subsequent divided kingdoms.

Daniel 2:36-43:

- Each section of the statue corresponds to a successive world empire, highlighting the transient nature of human kingdoms and the diversity of their strengths and weaknesses. The mixed iron and clay of the feet indicate a divided and unstable kingdom.

Daniel 2:44-45:

- The stone "cut out without hands" emphasizes the divine nature of the kingdom of God, which will ultimately overthrow all human empires. This eternal kingdom, inaugurated by the Messiah, will endure forever, fulfilling God's redemptive plan for humanity.

Theological Significance

The theological significance of Nebuchadnezzar's dream lies in its revelation of God's sovereignty, the transient nature of human power, and the ultimate establishment of God's eternal kingdom through the Messiah.

God's Sovereignty

The dream underscores God's control over history and His ability to raise and depose kingdoms according to His will. This theme is reiterated throughout the Book of Daniel, affirming God's supreme authority over earthly rulers.

Biblical References:

- Daniel 4:17: "This matter is by the decree of the watchers, and the demand by the word of the holy ones: to the intent that the living may know that the most High ruleth in the kingdom of men, and giveth it to whomsoever he will, and setteth up over it the basest of men."

- Romans 13:1: "Let every soul be subject unto the higher powers. For there is no power but of God: the powers that be are ordained of God."

The Messiah and the Kingdom of God

The stone represents the Messiah and His eternal kingdom, which will supersede all human empires. This prophetic vision aligns with New Testament teachings on the Kingdom of God and the role of Jesus as the cornerstone of this everlasting kingdom.

Biblical References:

- Psalm 118:22: "The stone which the builders refused is become the head stone of the corner."

- Matthew 21:42: "Jesus saith unto them, Did ye never read in the scriptures, The stone which the builders rejected, the same becomes the head of the corner: this is the Lord's doing, and it is marvelous in our eyes?"

Lessons for Believers

The vision of Nebuchadnezzar's dream offers several key lessons for believers today.

Trust in God's Sovereignty

Believers are encouraged to trust in God's sovereign control over history and the future. Despite the rise and fall of earthly powers, God's kingdom will ultimately prevail.

Faith in God's Plan

The detailed prophecy of world empires and their succession underscores the reliability of God's word and His prophetic revelations. Believers can have confidence in God's plan and His promises.

Hope in the Eternal Kingdom

The vision of the eternal kingdom provides hope and assurance for believers. The transient nature of human kingdoms contrasts with the permanence and righteousness of God's kingdom, offering a future anchored in divine promise.

Nebuchadnezzar's dream of the statue in Daniel 2 is a profound revelation of God's sovereignty, the transient nature of human kingdoms, and the ultimate establishment of God's eternal kingdom through the Messiah. This prophetic vision, interpreted by Daniel, underscores the themes of divine control, the reliability of God's word, and the hope of an everlasting kingdom.

As we reflect on this vision, may we be encouraged to trust in God's sovereignty, have faith in His prophetic revelations, and find hope in the promise of His eternal kingdom. The lessons from Nebuchadnezzar's dream continue to resonate, offering timeless truths and assurance for believers navigating the complexities of the world.

Interpretation by Daniel and the Messianic Kingdom

Daniel's interpretation of Nebuchadnezzar's dream of the statue in Daniel 2 provides profound insights into the future succession of world empires and the establishment of God's eternal kingdom. This interpretation not only reveals the transient nature of human kingdoms but also emphasizes the ultimate triumph of the Messianic kingdom. In this chapter, we will explore Daniel's interpretation and its implications for understanding the Messianic kingdom, using Bible verses, expository study, and exhaustive Strong's Concordance to provide comprehensive commentary and insights.

Daniel's Interpretation of the Dream

Daniel's recounting of Nebuchadnezzar's dream and its interpretation highlights the divine revelation given to him. This interpretation is crucial for understanding the prophetic timeline of world empires and the establishment of God's eternal kingdom.

The Dream Described

Daniel begins by recounting the dream in detail, describing the great statue composed of various materials:

"Thou, O king, sawest, and behold a great image. This great image, whose brightness was excellent, stood before thee; and the form thereof was terrible. This image's head was of fine gold, his breast and his arms of silver, his belly and his thighs of brass, His legs of iron, his feet part of iron and part of clay" (Daniel 2:31-33, KJV).

Key Elements of the Statue:

- Head of Gold: Represents the Babylonian Empire under Nebuchadnezzar.

- Chest and Arms of Silver: Symbolize the Medo-Persian Empire.

- Belly and Thighs of Bronze: Represent the Greek Empire.

- Legs of Iron: Depict the Roman Empire.

- Feet of Iron and Clay: Indicate a divided and unstable kingdom, often interpreted as the remnants of the Roman Empire or future divided kingdoms.

The Stone and the Great Mountain

The dream culminates with a stone that strikes the statue and becomes a great mountain:

"Thou sawest till that a stone was cut out without hands, which smote the image upon his feet that were of iron and clay, and brake them to pieces. Then was the iron, the clay, the brass, the silver, and the gold, broken to pieces together, and became like the chaff of the summer threshing floors; and the wind carried them away, that no place was found for them: and the stone that smote the image became a great mountain, and filled the whole earth" (Daniel 2:34-35, KJV).

Significance of the Stone:

- Divine Origin: The stone "cut out without hands" signifies divine origin, pointing to the Messianic kingdom.

- Destruction of Human Kingdoms: The stone's destruction of the statue represents the ultimate overthrow of human kingdoms by God's eternal kingdom.

- Establishment of the Eternal Kingdom: The stone becoming a great mountain symbolizes the expansive and eternal nature of God's kingdom.

Daniel's Interpretation

Daniel's interpretation provides a detailed explanation of the dream's symbolism and its prophetic significance:

"This is the dream; and we will tell the interpretation thereof before the king. Thou, O king, art a king of kings: for the God of heaven hath given thee a kingdom, power, and strength, and glory. And wheresoever the children of men dwell, the beasts of the field and the fowls of the heaven hath he given into thine hand and hath made thee ruler over them all. Thou art this head of gold" (Daniel 2:36-38, KJV).

Interpretation of the Statue:

- Head of Gold (Babylonian Empire): Nebuchadnezzar's reign is identified as the head of gold, symbolizing the Babylonian Empire's glory and power.

- Chest and Arms of Silver (Medo-Persian Empire): The succeeding empire, inferior to Babylon, represents the Medo-Persian Empire (Daniel 2:39).

- Belly and Thighs of Bronze (Greek Empire): The third empire, characterized by its widespread influence, represents the Greek Empire.

- Legs of Iron (Roman Empire): The fourth empire, known for its strength and dominance, represents the Roman Empire.

- Feet of Iron and Clay (Divided Kingdom): The mixture of iron and clay indicates a future divided and unstable kingdom, lacking the cohesion of previous empires (Daniel 2:41-43).

The Eternal Kingdom

The climax of the interpretation focuses on the establishment of God's eternal kingdom:

"And in the days of these kings shall the God of heaven set up a kingdom, which shall never be destroyed: and the kingdom shall not be left to other people, but it shall break in pieces and consume all these kingdoms, and it shall stand for ever. Forasmuch as thou sawest that the stone was cut out of the mountain without hands, and that it brake in pieces the iron, the brass, the clay, the silver, and the gold; the great God hath made known to the king what shall come to pass hereafter: and the dream is certain, and the interpretation thereof sure" (Daniel 2:44-45, KJV).

Key Elements of the Eternal Kingdom:

- Divine Establishment: The kingdom is set up by "the God of heaven," emphasizing its divine origin.

- Eternal Duration: The kingdom "shall never be destroyed," highlighting its everlasting nature.

- Supremacy Over Human Kingdoms: The kingdom will "break in pieces and consume all these kingdoms," indicating its ultimate victory over all earthly powers.

The Messianic Kingdom

The interpretation of Nebuchadnezzar's dream points to the future establishment of the Messianic kingdom, a central theme in biblical prophecy.

The Messiah as the Stone

The stone "cut out without hands" is a powerful symbol of the Messiah and His kingdom. This imagery aligns with other biblical references to the Messiah as a stone or cornerstone:

Biblical References:

- Psalm 118:22: "The stone which the builders refused is become the head stone of the corner."

- Isaiah 28:16: "Therefore thus saith the Lord GOD, Behold, I lay in Zion for a foundation a stone, a tried stone, a precious corner stone, a sure foundation: he that believeth shall not make haste."

- Matthew 21:42: "Jesus saith unto them, Did ye never read in the scriptures, The stone which the builders rejected, the same is become the head of the corner: this is the Lord's doing, and it is marvellous in our eyes?"

These references highlight the Messiah's role as the cornerstone of God's kingdom, a foundation that will endure forever.

The Nature of the Messianic Kingdom

The Messianic kingdom is characterized by its divine origin, eternal duration, and ultimate supremacy over all earthly kingdoms.

Key Characteristics:

- Divine Origin: The kingdom is established by God, emphasizing its divine nature and authority.

- Eternal Duration: Unlike human kingdoms, the Messianic kingdom will last forever, fulfilling God's promise of everlasting dominion (Daniel 7:14).

- Supremacy Over Earthly Kingdoms: The Messianic kingdom will triumph over all human powers, establishing justice, peace, and righteousness.

Fulfillment in Christ

The New Testament reveals Jesus Christ as the fulfillment of the Messianic kingdom prophesied in Daniel 2. Jesus' ministry, death, and resurrection inaugurate the kingdom of God, which will be fully realized at His second coming.

Biblical References:

- Mark 1:15: "The time is fulfilled, and the kingdom of God is at hand: repent ye, and believe the gospel."

- Luke 1:32-33: "He shall be great, and shall be called the Son of the Highest: and the Lord God shall give unto him the throne of his father David: And he shall reign over the house of Jacob for ever; and of his kingdom there shall be no end."

- Revelation 11:15: "And the seventh angel sounded; and there were great voices in heaven, saying, The kingdoms of this world become the kingdoms of our Lord and of his Christ, and he shall reign forever and ever."

Expository Analysis and Strong's Concordance

Using Strong's Concordance, we can gain deeper insights into the key terms and concepts in Daniel's interpretation and the Messianic kingdom.

Key Terms

- Kingdom (מַלְכוּ, malku, Strong's H4437): Refers to the various empires represented by the different parts of the statue and the ultimate kingdom of God.

- Stone (אֶבֶן, eben, Strong's H68): Represents the Messiah and the kingdom of God, "cut out without hands," indicating divine origin.

- Great Mountain (הַר גָּדוֹל, har gadol, Strong's H2022): Symbolizes the expansive and eternal nature of God's kingdom.

Comprehensive Commentary

Daniel 2:36-38:

- The identification of Nebuchadnezzar as the head of gold underscores the glory and power of the Babylonian Empire. Daniel emphasizes that this power is given by God, highlighting divine sovereignty.

Daniel 2:39-43:

- The succession of empires (Medo-Persian, Greek, and Roman) illustrates the transient nature of human kingdoms. The mixture of iron and clay in the feet represents a future-divided kingdom, emphasizing instability and lack of cohesion.

Daniel 2:44-45:- The stone's divine origin and its destruction of the statue symbolize the Messianic kingdom's ultimate victory over all human powers. This eternal kingdom, established by God, will endure forever and bring about the fulfillment of God's redemptive plan.

Theological Significance

The theological significance of Daniel's interpretation lies in its revelation of God's sovereignty, the transient nature of human power, and the ultimate establishment of God's eternal kingdom through the Messiah.

God's Sovereignty

The dream underscores God's control over history and His ability to raise and depose kingdoms according to His will. This theme is reiterated throughout the Book of Daniel, affirming God's supreme authority over earthly rulers.

Biblical References:

- Daniel 4:17: "This matter is by the decree of the watchers, and the demand by the word of the holy ones: to the intent that the living may know that the most High ruleth in the kingdom of men, and giveth it to whomsoever he will, and setteth up over it the basest of men."

- Romans 13:1: "Let every soul be subject unto the higher powers. For there is no power but of God: the powers that be are ordained of God."

The Messiah and the Kingdom of God

The stone represents the Messiah and His eternal kingdom, which will supersede all human empires. This prophetic vision aligns with New Testament teachings on the Kingdom of God and the role of Jesus as the cornerstone of this everlasting kingdom.

Biblical References:

- Psalm 118:22: "The stone which the builders refused is become the head stone of the corner."

- Matthew 21:42: "Jesus saith unto them, Did ye never read in the scriptures, The stone which the builders rejected, the same becomes the head of the corner: this is the Lord's doing, and it is marvelous in our eyes?"

- 1 Peter 2:6: "Wherefore also it is contained in the scripture, Behold, I lay in Sion a chief cornerstone, elect, precious: and he that believeth on him shall not be confounded."

Lessons for Believers

The interpretation of Nebuchadnezzar's dream and the revelation of the Messianic kingdom offer several key lessons for believers today.

Trust in God's Sovereignty

Believers are encouraged to trust in God's sovereign control over history and the future. Despite the rise and fall of earthly powers, God's kingdom will ultimately prevail.

Faith in God's Plan

The detailed prophecy of world empires and their succession underscores the reliability of God's word and His prophetic revelations. Believers can have confidence in God's plan and His promises.

Hope in the Eternal Kingdom

The vision of the eternal kingdom provides hope and assurance for believers. The transient nature of human kingdoms contrasts with the permanence and righteousness of God's kingdom, offering a future anchored in divine promise.

Daniel's interpretation of Nebuchadnezzar's dream in Daniel 2 is a profound revelation of God's sovereignty, the transient nature of human kingdoms, and the ultimate establishment of God's eternal kingdom through the Messiah. This prophetic vision, interpreted by Daniel, underscores the themes of divine control, the reliability of God's word, and the hope of an everlasting kingdom.

As we reflect on this interpretation, may we be encouraged to trust in God's sovereignty, have faith in His prophetic revelations, and find hope in the promise of His eternal kingdom. The lessons from Nebuchadnezzar's dream continue to resonate, offering timeless truths and assurance for believers navigating the complexities of the world.

Jesus as the Stone That Becomes a Great Mountain

The dream of Nebuchadnezzar, as interpreted by Daniel in Daniel 2, provides a vivid and prophetic picture of the future succession of world empires and the ultimate establishment of God's eternal kingdom. Central to this vision is the stone "cut out without hands" that strikes the statue, breaking it to pieces, and then grows into a great mountain that fills the whole earth. This stone symbolizes Jesus Christ and His Messianic kingdom. In this chapter, we will explore the significance of Jesus as the stone that becomes a great mountain, using Bible verses, expository study, and exhaustive Strong's Concordance to provide comprehensive commentary and insights.

The Stone in Nebuchadnezzar's Dream

The Dream Described

Nebuchadnezzar's dream features a magnificent statue composed of various materials, each representing successive world empires:

"Thou, O king, sawest, and behold a great image. This great image, whose brightness was excellent, stood before thee; and the form thereof was terrible. This image's head was of fine gold, his breast and his arms of silver, his belly and his thighs of brass, His legs of iron, his feet part of iron and part of clay. Thou sawest till that a stone was cut out without hands, which smote the image upon his feet that were of iron and clay, and brake them to pieces" (Daniel 2:31-34, KJV).

The Stone's Action

The stone's action in the dream is both destructive and transformative:

- Matthew 21:42: "Jesus said to them, 'Have you never read in the Scriptures: The stone which the builders rejected, this became the chief corner stone; this came about from the Lord, and it is marvelous in our eyes'?"

- 1 Peter 2:6: "For this is contained in Scripture: 'Behold, I lay in Zion a choice stone, a precious cornerstone, and he who believes in Him will not be disappointed.'"

Lessons for Believers

The interpretation of Nebuchadnezzar's dream and the revelation of the Messianic kingdom offer several key lessons for believers today.

Trust in God's Sovereignty

Believers are encouraged to trust in God's sovereign control over history and the future. Despite the rise and fall of earthly powers, God's kingdom will ultimately prevail.

Faith in God's Plan

The detailed prophecy of world empires and their succession underscores the reliability of God's word and His prophetic revelations. Believers can have confidence in God's plan and His promises.

Hope in the Eternal Kingdom

The vision of the eternal kingdom provides hope and assurance for believers. The transient nature of human kingdoms contrasts with the permanence and righteousness of God's kingdom, offering a future anchored in divine promise.

Daniel's interpretation of Nebuchadnezzar's dream in Daniel 2 is a profound revelation of God's sovereignty, the transient nature of human kingdoms, and the ultimate establishment of God's eternal kingdom through the Messiah. This prophetic vision, interpreted by Daniel, underscores the themes of divine control, the reliability of God's word, and the hope of an everlasting kingdom.

As we reflect on this interpretation, may we be encouraged to trust in God's sovereignty, have faith in His prophetic revelations, and find hope in the promise of His eternal kingdom. The lessons from Nebuchadnezzar's dream continue to resonate, offering timeless truths and assurance for believers navigating the complexities of the world.

Jesus as the Stone That Becomes a Great Mountain

The dream of Nebuchadnezzar, as interpreted by Daniel in Daniel 2, provides a vivid and prophetic picture of the future succession of world empires and the ultimate establishment of God's eternal kingdom. Central to this vision is the stone "cut out without hands" that strikes the statue, breaking it to pieces, and then grows into a great mountain that fills the whole earth. This stone symbolizes Jesus Christ and His Messianic kingdom. In this chapter, we will explore the significance of Jesus as the stone that becomes a great mountain, using Bible verses, expository study, and exhaustive Strong's Concordance to provide comprehensive commentary and insights."Then was the iron, the clay, the brass, the silver, and the gold, broken to pieces together, and became like the chaff of the summer threshing floors; and the wind carried them away, that no place was found for them: and the stone that smote the image became a great mountain, and filled the whole earth" (Daniel 2:35, KJV).

Key Elements:

- Destruction of the Statue: The stone strikes the statue's feet of iron and clay, causing the entire statue to collapse and be reduced to chaff.

- Transformation into a Great Mountain: The stone then grows into a great mountain that fills the entire earth, symbolizing the establishment of an eternal kingdom.

Interpretation by Daniel

Daniel's interpretation of the dream reveals the prophetic significance of the stone and its role in the divine plan:

"And in the days of these kings shall the God of heaven set up a kingdom, which shall never be destroyed: and the kingdom shall not be left to other people, but it shall break in pieces and consume all these kingdoms, and it shall stand forever. Forasmuch as thou sawest that the stone was cut out of the mountain without hands and that it brake in pieces the iron, the brass, the clay, the silver, and the gold; the great God hath made known to the king what shall come to pass hereafter: and the dream is certain, and the interpretation thereof sure" (Daniel 2:44-45, KJV).

Key Elements of the Interpretation:

- Divine Establishment: The stone represents a kingdom established by God, not by human hands.

- Eternal Duration: This kingdom will never be destroyed and will last forever.

- Supremacy Over Human Kingdoms: The stone's destruction of the statue signifies the ultimate triumph of God's kingdom over all earthly powers.

Jesus as the Stone

Biblical References to Jesus as the Stone

The imagery of the stone is a recurring motif in the Bible, often associated with the Messiah. Jesus Christ is frequently identified as the stone or cornerstone in both the Old and New Testaments.

Old Testament References:

- Psalm 118:22: "The stone which the builders refused is become the head stone of the corner."

- Isaiah 28:16: "Therefore thus saith the Lord GOD, Behold, I lay in Zion for a foundation a stone, a tried stone, a precious corner stone, a sure foundation: he that believeth shall not make haste."

New Testament References:

- Matthew 21:42: "Jesus saith unto them, Did ye never read in the scriptures, The stone which the builders rejected, the same is become the head of the corner: this is the Lord's doing, and it is marvellous in our eyes?"

- Acts 4:11: "This is the stone which was set at naught of you builders, which is become the head of the corner."

- 1 Peter 2:6: "Wherefore also it is contained in the scripture, Behold, I lay in Sion a chief cornerstone, elect, precious: and he that believeth on him shall not be confounded."

The Stone "Cut Out Without Hands"

The phrase "cut out without hands" emphasizes the divine origin and nature of the stone, pointing to Jesus Christ as the divinely appointed Savior and King.

Divine Origin:

- John 1:1-2, 14: "In the beginning was the Word, and the Word was with God, and the Word was God. The same was in the beginning with God… And the Word was made flesh, and dwelt among us, and we beheld his glory, the glory as of the only begotten of the Father, full of grace and truth."

- Hebrews 1:3: "Who being the brightness of his glory, and the express image of his person, and upholding all things by the word of his power, when he had by himself purged our sins, sat down on the right hand of the Majesty on high."

The Messianic Kingdom

Establishment of the Kingdom

Jesus' ministry, death, and resurrection inaugurated the Kingdom of God, fulfilling the prophecy of the stone that becomes a great mountain.

Biblical References:

- Mark 1:15: "The time is fulfilled, and the kingdom of God is at hand: repent ye, and believe the gospel."

- Luke 17:20-21: "And when he was demanded of the Pharisees when the kingdom of God should come, he answered them and said, The kingdom of God cometh not with observation: Neither shall they say, Lo here! or, lo there! for, behold, the kingdom of God is within you."

Eternal Duration and Supremacy

The Messianic kingdom is characterized by its eternal nature and ultimate supremacy over all earthly powers.

Eternal Duration:

- Daniel 7:14: "And there was given him dominion, and glory, and a kingdom, that all people, nations, and languages, should serve him: his dominion is an everlasting dominion, which shall not pass away, and his kingdom that which shall not be destroyed."

- Revelation 11:15: "And the seventh angel sounded; and there were great voices in heaven, saying, The kingdoms of this world become the kingdoms of our Lord, and of his Christ; and he shall reign for ever and ever."

Supremacy Over Earthly Kingdoms:

- Philippians 2:9-11: "Wherefore God also hath highly exalted him, and given him a name which is above every name: That at the name of Jesus every knee should bow, of things in heaven, and things in earth, and things under the earth; And that every tongue should confess that Jesus Christ is Lord, to the glory of God the Father."

- Revelation 19:16: "And he hath on his vesture and on his thigh a name written, KING OF KINGS, AND LORD OF LORDS."

Expository Analysis and Strong's Concordance

Using Strong's Concordance, we can gain deeper insights into the key terms and concepts in this prophetic vision.

Key Terms

- Stone (אֶבֶן, eben, Strong's H68): Represents the Messiah and the kingdom of God, "cut out without hands," indicating divine origin.

- Kingdom (מַלְכוּ, malku, Strong's H4437): Refers to the various empires represented by the different parts of the statue and the ultimate kingdom of God.

- Great Mountain (הַר גָּדוֹל, har gadol, Strong's H2022): Symbolizes the expansive and eternal nature of God's kingdom.

Comprehensive Commentary

Daniel 2:34-35:

- The stone's action of striking the statue and breaking it to pieces symbolizes the decisive and transformative impact of Christ's kingdom on human history. The subsequent growth into a great mountain signifies the universal and eternal nature of His reign.

Daniel 2:44-45:

- The divine origin and eternal duration of the kingdom established by the stone underscore the fulfillment of Messianic prophecies. This kingdom, unlike human empires, will stand forever and bring about the ultimate realization of God's redemptive plan.

Theological Significance

The theological significance of Jesus as the stone that becomes a great mountain lies in His role as the foundation of God's eternal kingdom and the fulfillment of divine prophecy.

Jesus as the Cornerstone

The imagery of Jesus as the cornerstone highlights His foundational role in God's redemptive plan and the establishment of His kingdom.

Biblical References:

- Ephesians 2:19-22: "Now therefore ye are no more strangers and foreigners, but fellowcitizens with the saints, and of the household of God; And are built upon the foundation of the apostles and prophets, Jesus Christ himself being the chief corner stone; In whom all the building fitly framed together groweth unto an holy temple in the Lord: In whom ye also are builded together for an habitation of God through the Spirit."

The Inauguration of the Kingdom

Jesus' earthly ministry, death, and resurrection inaugurated the Kingdom of God, fulfilling the prophecy of the stone that becomes a great mountain.

Biblical References:

- Colossians 1:13: "Who hath delivered us from the power of darkness, and hath translated us into the kingdom of his dear Son."

- Hebrews 12:28: "Wherefore we receiving a kingdom which cannot be moved, let us have grace, whereby we may serve God acceptably with reverence and godly fear."

Lessons for Believers

The prophecy of Jesus as the stone that becomes a great mountain offers several key lessons for believers today.

Trust in Jesus as the Foundation

Believers are encouraged to build their lives on the foundation of Jesus Christ, the cornerstone of their faith and the eternal kingdom.

Confidence in the Eternal Kingdom

The assurance of the eternal nature of God's kingdom provides hope and confidence for believers, knowing that they are part of an unshakeable and everlasting dominion.

Active Participation in the Kingdom

Believers are called to actively participate in the growth and expansion of God's kingdom, sharing the gospel and living out the values of the kingdom in their daily lives.

The prophecy of Nebuchadnezzar's dream in Daniel 2, and its interpretation by Daniel, vividly portrays Jesus as the stone that becomes a great mountain. This imagery highlights Jesus' foundational role in God's eternal kingdom and the fulfillment of divine prophecy. As we reflect on this vision, may we be encouraged to trust in Jesus as the cornerstone, find confidence in the assurance of His eternal kingdom, and actively participate in its growth and expansion. The lessons from this prophetic vision continue to resonate, offering timeless truths and hope for believers navigating the complexities of the world.

CHAPTER 04

THE SON OF MAN

The vision of the four beasts and the Son of Man in Daniel 7 is one of the most profound and significant prophetic revelations in the Old Testament. This vision not only provides insights into the rise and fall of world empires but also introduces the figure of the Son of Man, a Messianic title that Jesus Christ would later claim for Himself. In this chapter, we will explore the vision in detail, examining its elements, interpretation, and the theological significance of the Son of Man. We will use Bible verses, expository study, and exhaustive Strong's Concordance to provide comprehensive commentary and insights.

The Vision of the Four Beasts

The Four Beasts Described

Daniel's vision begins with the emergence of four great beasts from the sea, each representing a kingdom that will emerge on the earth. This vision is recorded in Daniel 7:1-8.

The First Beast: The Lion with Eagle's Wings

"The first was like a lion, and had eagle's wings: I beheld till the wings thereof were plucked, and it was lifted up from the earth, and made stand upon the feet as a man, and a man's heart was given to it" (Daniel 7:4, KJV).

Key Elements:

- Lion with Eagle's Wings: Represents the Babylonian Empire, known for its power and swiftness.

- Wings Plucked: Symbolizes the humbling of Babylon, possibly reflecting Nebuchadnezzar's period of insanity (Daniel 4).

- Human Heart Given: Indicates a transformation or humanization of the kingdom, again reflective of Nebuchadnezzar's restoration.

Strong's Concordance:

- Lion (אַרְיֵה, aryeh, Strong's H744): Symbol of strength and dominance.

- Wings (גַּף, gap, Strong's H1611): Symbol of swiftness and mobility.

The Second Beast: The Bear

"And behold another beast, a second, like to a bear, and it raised up itself on one side, and it had three ribs in the mouth of it between the teeth of it: and they said thus unto it, Arise, devour much flesh" (Daniel 7:5, KJV).

Key Elements:

- Bear: Represents the Medo-Persian Empire, known for its military strength and conquests.

- Raised Up on One Side: Indicates the dominance of the Persian part of the empire over the Median.

- Three Ribs: Symbolizes the major conquests of the Medo-Persian Empire, likely Babylon, Lydia, and Egypt.

Strong's Concordance:

- Bear (דֹּב, dob, Strong's H1678): Symbol of power and ferocity.

- Ribs (עֲלַע, 'al'el, Strong's H5967): Indicates the spoils or conquests held by the beast.

The Third Beast: The Leopard with Four Wings and Four Heads

"After this I beheld, and lo another, like a leopard, which had upon the back of it four wings of a fowl; the beast had also four heads; and dominion was given to it" (Daniel 7:6, KJV).

Key Elements:

- Leopard with Four Wings: Represents the Greek Empire under Alexander the Great, known for its rapid conquests.

- Four Heads: Symbolizes the division of the Greek Empire into four parts after Alexander's death.

Strong's Concordance:

- Leopard (נָמֵר, namer, Strong's H5245): Symbol of swiftness and agility.

- Wings (כָּנָף, kanaph, Strong's H3671): Emphasizes speed and mobility.

- Heads (רֹאשׁ, rosh, Strong's H7218): Represents authority and leadership.

The Fourth Beast: The Terrifying and Powerful Beast

"After this I saw in the night visions, and behold a fourth beast, dreadful and terrible, and strong exceedingly; and it had great iron teeth: it devoured and brake in pieces, and stamped the residue with the feet of it: and it was diverse from all the beasts that were before it; and it had ten horns" (Daniel 7:7, KJV).

Key Elements:

- Terrifying Beast: Represents the Roman Empire, known for its unprecedented power and brutality.

- Iron Teeth: Symbolizes its strength and ability to crush opposition.

- Ten Horns: Represents ten kings or kingdoms that would emerge from this empire.

Strong's Concordance:

- Beast (חֵיוָה, cheyva, Strong's H2423): Represents kingdoms or empires.

- Horns (קֶרֶן, qeren, Strong's H7161): Symbolizes power and authority.

The Little Horn

"I considered the horns, and, behold, there came up among them another little horn, before whom there were three of the first horns plucked up by the roots: and, behold, in this horn were eyes like the eyes of man, and a mouth speaking great things" (Daniel 7:8, KJV).

Key Elements:

- Little Horn: Represents a future ruler or kingdom that will arise from the remnants of the Roman Empire.

- Eyes of a Man: Indicates intelligence or insight.

- Mouth Speaking Great Things: Symbolizes arrogance and blasphemy.

Strong's Concordance:

- Horn (קֶרֶן, qeren, Strong's H7161): Symbolizes power and authority.

The Vision of the Son of Man

The Heavenly Court

Following the vision of the four beasts, Daniel sees a heavenly court where the Ancient of Days takes His seat:

"I beheld till the thrones were cast down, and the Ancient of days did sit, whose garment was white as snow, and the hair of his head like the pure wool: his throne was like the fiery flame, and his wheels as burning fire" (Daniel 7:9, KJV).

Key Elements:

- Ancient of Days: Represents God, characterized by purity and wisdom.

- Fiery Throne: Symbolizes divine judgment and power.

Strong's Concordance:

- Ancient (עַתִּיק, attiq, Strong's H6268): Indicates eternal existence.

- Throne (כָּרְסֵא, karse, Strong's H3764): Represents authority and sovereignty.

The Judgment and Destruction of the Fourth Beast

The fourth beast is judged and destroyed, symbolizing the end of earthly kingdoms that oppose God's rule:

"I beheld then because of the voice of the great words which the horn spake: I beheld even till the beast was slain, and his body destroyed, and given to the burning flame" (Daniel 7:11, KJV).

Key Elements:

- Judgment: Represents God's ultimate authority over earthly powers.

- Destruction of the Beast: Symbolizes the final defeat of evil empires.

The Son of Man

The vision culminates with the appearance of the Son of Man, who is given eternal dominion and authority:

"I saw in the night visions, and, behold, one like the Son of man came with the clouds of heaven, and came to the Ancient of days, and they brought him near before him. And there was given him dominion, and glory, and a kingdom, that all people, nations, and languages, should serve him: his dominion is an everlasting dominion, which shall not pass away, and his kingdom that which shall not be destroyed" (Daniel 7:13-14, KJV).

Key Elements:

- Son of Man: A Messianic title later claimed by Jesus.

- Clouds of Heaven: Symbolizes divine presence and authority.

- Everlasting Dominion: Represents the eternal reign of the Messiah.

Strong's Concordance:

- Son (בַּר, bar, Strong's H1247): Indicates a human descendant.

- Man (אֱנָשׁ, enash, Strong's H606): Emphasizes humanity.

- Dominion (שָׁלְטָן, sholtan, Strong's H7985): Symbolizes sovereign authority.

Interpretation and Theological Significance

The Interpretation of the Vision

Daniel's vision is interpreted by a heavenly being, revealing the meaning of the four beasts and the significance of the Son of Man:

"These great beasts, which are four, are four kings, which shall arise out of the earth. But the saints of the most High shall take the kingdom, and possess the kingdom for ever, even for ever and ever" (Daniel 7:17-18, KJV).

Key Elements:

- Four Kings: Represents the four successive world empires.

- Saints of the Most High: Represents the people of God who will inherit the eternal kingdom.

The Son of Man in the New Testament

Jesus frequently referred to Himself as the Son of Man, directly linking His ministry and mission to this vision in Daniel.

Biblical References:

- Matthew 24:30: "And then shall appear the sign of the Son of man in heaven: and then shall all the tribes of the earth mourn, and they shall see the Son of man coming in the clouds of heaven with power and great glory."

- Mark 14:61-62: "But he held his peace, and answered nothing. Again the high priest asked him, and said unto him, Art thou the Christ, the Son of the Blessed? And Jesus said, I am: and ye shall see the Son of man sitting on the right hand of power, and coming in the clouds of heaven."

- Revelation 1:13: "And in the midst of the seven candlesticks one like unto the Son of man, clothed with a garment down to the foot, and girt about the paps with a golden girdle."

Theological Significance

The vision of the Son of Man emphasizes several key theological themes:

Divine Authority: The Son of Man is given dominion, glory, and a kingdom by the Ancient of Days, signifying divine authority and approval.

Eternal Reign: The kingdom of the Son of Man is eternal, contrasting with the transient nature of earthly kingdoms. This eternal reign fulfills the promises of an everlasting kingdom found throughout the Old Testament.

Inclusivity: The kingdom of the Son of Man includes all peoples, nations, and languages, highlighting the universal scope of God's redemptive plan.

Judgment and Victory: The vision concludes with the judgment and destruction of the fourth beast, symbolizing the ultimate victory of God's kingdom over evil.

Lessons for Believers

The vision of the four beasts and the Son of Man offers several key lessons for believers today.

Trust in Divine Sovereignty

Believers are encouraged to trust in God's sovereignty over history and the future. Despite the rise and fall of earthly powers, God's kingdom will ultimately prevail.

Hope in the Eternal Kingdom

The assurance of the eternal nature of the Son of Man's kingdom provides hope and confidence for believers, knowing that they are part of an unshakeable and everlasting dominion.

Active Participation in God's Kingdom

Believers are called to actively participate in the advancement of God's kingdom, sharing the gospel and living out the values of the kingdom in their daily lives.

The vision of the four beasts and the Son of Man in Daniel 7 is a profound revelation of God's sovereignty, the transient nature of human kingdoms, and the ultimate establishment of the eternal kingdom through the Messiah. The figure of the Son of Man, later claimed by Jesus, highlights the fulfillment of this prophetic vision and emphasizes the themes of divine authority, eternal reign, inclusivity, and ultimate victory.

As we reflect on this vision, may we be encouraged to trust in God's sovereignty, find hope in the assurance of His eternal kingdom, and actively participate in its growth and expansion. The lessons from this prophetic vision continue to resonate, offering timeless truths and hope for believers navigating the complexities of the world.

Jesus' Reference to Himself as the Son of Man

One of the most profound titles that Jesus used to describe Himself is "the Son of Man." This title, deeply rooted in the prophetic vision of Daniel 7, carries significant theological implications and reveals key aspects of Jesus' identity and mission. In this chapter, we will explore Jesus' use of the title "Son of Man," its Old Testament background, and its implications for understanding His person and work. We will use Bible verses, expository study, and exhaustive Strong's Concordance to provide comprehensive commentary and insights.

The Old Testament Background: The Son of Man in Daniel 7

In Daniel 7, the vision of the four beasts culminates with the appearance of a figure described as "one like the Son of man," who is given dominion, glory, and an everlasting kingdom:

"I saw in the night visions, and, behold, one like the Son of man came with the clouds of heaven, and came to the Ancient of days, and they brought him near before him. And there was given him dominion, and glory, and a kingdom, that all people, nations, and languages, should serve him: his dominion is an everlasting dominion, which shall not pass away, and his kingdom that which shall not be destroyed" (Daniel 7:13-14, KJV).

Key Elements:

- Son of Man: A Messianic figure with divine authority.

- Clouds of Heaven: Symbolizes divine presence and majesty.

- Everlasting Dominion: Represents an eternal and universal kingdom.

Strong's Concordance:

- Son (בַּר, bar, Strong's H1247): Indicates a human descendant.

- Man (אֱנָשׁ, enash, Strong's H606): Emphasizes humanity.

- Dominion (שָׁלְטָן, sholtan, Strong's H7985): Symbolizes sovereign authority.

Jesus' Use of the Title "Son of Man"

Jesus frequently referred to Himself as the "Son of Man," directly linking His ministry and mission to the vision in Daniel 7. This title is used over 80 times in the Gospels and is key to understanding Jesus' self-identity and His role in God's redemptive plan.

Jesus' Authority and Mission

Jesus used the title "Son of Man" to emphasize His authority and divine mission.

Forgiveness of Sins:

- Matthew 9:6: "But that ye may know that the Son of man hath power on earth to forgive sins, (then saith he to the sick of the palsy,) Arise, take up thy bed, and go unto thine house."

- Mark 2:10: "But that ye may know that the Son of man hath power on earth to forgive sins, (he saith to the sick of the palsy,)"

Lord of the Sabbath:

- Mark 2:28: "Therefore the Son of man is Lord also of the sabbath."

- Matthew 12:8: "For the Son of man is Lord even of the sabbath day."

Jesus' Suffering and Death

Jesus also used the title to predict His suffering, death, and resurrection, highlighting His role as the suffering servant.

Prediction of Suffering:

- Mark 8:31: "And he began to teach them, that the Son of man must suffer many things, and be rejected of the elders, and of the chief priests, and scribes, and be killed, and after three days rise again."

- Matthew 17:12: "But I say unto you, That Elias is come already, and they knew him not, but have done unto him whatsoever they listed. Likewise shall also the Son of man suffer of them."

Crucifixion and Resurrection:

- Matthew 20:18-19: "Behold, we go up to Jerusalem; and the Son of man shall be betrayed unto the chief priests and unto the scribes, and they shall condemn him to death, And shall deliver him to the Gentiles to mock, and to scourge, and to crucify him: and the third day he shall rise again."

- Luke 24:7: "Saying, The Son of man must be delivered into the hands of sinful men, and be crucified, and the third day rise again."

Jesus' Eschatological Role

Jesus referred to Himself as the Son of Man in the context of His second coming and final judgment, underscoring His role in the eschatological fulfillment of God's kingdom.

Coming in Glory:

- Matthew 24:30: "And then shall appear the sign of the Son of man in heaven: and then shall all the tribes of the earth mourn, and they shall see the Son of man coming in the clouds of heaven with power and great glory."

- Mark 13:26: "And then shall they see the Son of man coming in the clouds with great power and glory."

Final Judgment:

- Matthew 25:31-32: "When the Son of man shall come in his glory, and all the holy angels with him, then shall he sit upon the throne of his glory: And before him shall be gathered all nations: and he shall separate them one from another, as a shepherd divideth his sheep from the goats."

- John 5:27: "And hath given him authority to execute judgment also, because he is the Son of man."

Theological Significance of the Title "Son of Man"

Humanity and Divinity

The title "Son of Man" encapsulates the paradox of Jesus' identity as both fully human and fully divine. By using this title, Jesus emphasizes His solidarity with humanity while also asserting His divine authority and messianic mission.

Biblical References:

- Philippians 2:6-8: "Who, being in the form of God, thought it not robbery to be equal with God: But made himself of no reputation, and took upon him the form of a servant, and was made in the likeness of men: And being found in fashion as a man, he humbled himself, and became obedient unto death, even the death of the cross."

- John 1:14: "And the Word was made flesh, and dwelt among us, and we beheld his glory, the glory as of the only begotten of the Father, full of grace and truth."

Suffering Servant

The title also connects Jesus to the suffering servant motif found in Isaiah. Jesus' reference to Himself as the Son of Man who must suffer and die aligns with the prophecies of a servant who would bear the sins of many.

Biblical References:

- Isaiah 53:3-5: "He is despised and rejected of men; a man of sorrows, and acquainted with grief: and we hid as it were our faces from him; he was despised, and we esteemed him not. Surely he hath borne our griefs, and carried our sorrows: yet we did esteem him stricken, smitten of God, and afflicted. But he was wounded for our transgressions, he was bruised for our iniquities: the chastisement of our peace was upon him; and with his stripes we are healed."

- Matthew 26:64: "Jesus saith unto him, Thou hast said: nevertheless I say unto you, Hereafter shall ye see the Son of man sitting on the right hand of power, and coming in the clouds of heaven."

Eschatological Judge

Jesus' references to the Son of Man in the context of His second coming and final judgment highlight His role as the eschatological judge who will bring God's kingdom to its ultimate fulfillment.

Biblical References:

- Revelation 14:14: "And I looked, and behold a white cloud, and upon the cloud one sat like unto the Son of man, having on his head a golden crown, and in his hand a sharp sickle."

- Matthew 13:41-43: "The Son of man shall send forth his angels, and they shall gather out of his kingdom all things that offend, and them which do iniquity; And shall cast them into a furnace of fire: there shall be wailing and gnashing of teeth. Then shall the righteous shine forth as the sun in the kingdom of their Father. Who hath ears to hear, let him hear."

Expository Analysis and Strong's Concordance

Using Strong's Concordance, we can delve deeper into the significance of the title "Son of Man" and its implications.

Key Terms

- Son (בַּר, bar, Strong's H1247): Indicates a human descendant.

- Man (אֱנָשׁ, enash, Strong's H606): Emphasizes humanity.

- Dominion (שָׁלְטָן, sholtan, Strong's H7985): Symbolizes sovereign authority.

Comprehensive Commentary

Daniel 7:13-14:

- The vision of the Son of Man coming with the clouds of heaven and receiving dominion, glory, and an everlasting kingdom establishes the Messianic expectations that Jesus fulfills. This passage sets the stage for understanding Jesus' use of the title and its implications for His identity and mission.

Matthew 24:30:

- Jesus' reference to the Son of Man coming in the clouds of heaven ties directly to Daniel's vision, emphasizing His divine authority and the fulfillment of prophetic expectations.

Philippians 2:6-8:

- This passage highlights the dual nature of Jesus as both divine and human, which is encapsulated in the title "Son of Man." Jesus' humility and obedience unto death are central to His mission and identity.

Lessons for Believers

Embrace the Fullness of Jesus' Identity

Believers are encouraged to embrace the fullness of Jesus' identity as both fully human and fully divine. The title "Son of Man" invites us to understand and appreciate the depth of His incarnation and His solidarity with humanity.

Follow the Suffering Servant

Jesus' use of the title "Son of Man" in the context of His suffering and death challenges believers to follow His example of humility, obedience, and self-sacrifice. We are called to take up our cross and follow Him, embracing the path of the suffering servant.

Anticipate the Coming Kingdom

The eschatological implications of the title "Son of Man" remind believers to live with a sense of anticipation and hope for the coming kingdom. We are called to be vigilant and faithful, knowing that Jesus will return in glory to judge the living and the dead and to establish His everlasting dominion.

Jesus' reference to Himself as the "Son of Man" is a profound declaration of His identity and mission. Rooted in the prophetic vision of Daniel 7, this title encapsulates His humanity, divinity, role as the suffering servant, and eschatological judge. As we reflect on Jesus' use of this title, may we be encouraged to embrace the fullness of His identity, follow His example of humility and obedience, and live with hope and anticipation for His coming kingdom. The lessons from Jesus' reference to Himself as the Son of Man continue to resonate, offering timeless truths and hope for believers navigating the complexities of the world.

The Eternal Dominion and Divine Authority of Christ

Central to the Christian faith is the belief in the eternal dominion and divine authority of Jesus Christ. This concept is deeply rooted in the Old and New Testaments, particularly in the prophetic vision of Daniel 7, where the "Son of Man" is given everlasting dominion and authority. In this chapter, we will explore the biblical foundation of Christ's eternal dominion and divine authority, examining how these themes are presented in Scripture and their implications for believers today.

The Prophetic Vision in Daniel 7

The Vision of the Son of Man

The vision of the Son of Man in Daniel 7 is a pivotal passage that introduces the theme of eternal dominion and divine authority.

Daniel 7:13-14:

"I saw in the night visions, and, behold, one like the Son of man came with the clouds of heaven, and came to the Ancient of days, and they brought him near before him. And there was given him dominion, and glory, and a kingdom, that all people, nations, and languages, should serve him: his dominion is an everlasting dominion, which shall not pass away, and his kingdom that which shall not be destroyed."

Key Elements:

- Son of Man: A Messianic figure who receives divine authority.

- Clouds of Heaven: Symbolizes divine presence and majesty.

- Everlasting Dominion: Represents an eternal and universal reign.

Strong's Concordance:

- Dominion (שָׁלְטָן, sholtan, Strong's H7985): Symbolizes sovereign authority.

- Glory (יְקָר, yeqar, Strong's H3367): Indicates honor and majesty.

- Kingdom (מַלְכוּ, malku, Strong's H4437): Represents the realm over which the Son of Man will rule.

Interpretation of the Vision

The interpretation of Daniel's vision reveals the significance of the eternal dominion and authority given to the Son of Man.

Daniel 7:17-18:

"These great beasts, which are four, are four kings, which shall arise out of the earth. But the saints of the most High shall take the kingdom, and possess the kingdom for ever, even for ever and ever."

Daniel 7:27:

"And the kingdom and dominion, and the greatness of the kingdom under the whole heaven, shall be given to the people of the saints of the most High, whose kingdom is an everlasting kingdom, and all dominions shall serve and obey him."

Key Elements:

- Four Kings: Represents successive world empires.

- Saints of the Most High: Refers to God's people who will inherit the eternal kingdom.

- Everlasting Kingdom: Emphasizes the eternal nature of the Messianic reign.

Christ's Eternal Dominion in the New Testament

The Authority of Jesus

The New Testament frequently affirms the divine authority and eternal dominion of Jesus Christ, highlighting His fulfillment of the Messianic prophecy in Daniel.

Matthew 28:18:

"And Jesus came and spake unto them, saying, All power is given unto me in heaven and in earth."

Key Elements:

- All Power: Indicates Jesus' comprehensive authority over all creation.

- Heaven and Earth: Emphasizes the universal scope of His dominion.

Strong's Concordance:

- Power (ἐξουσία, exousia, Strong's G1849): Symbolizes authority and jurisdiction.

The Everlasting Kingdom

Jesus' teachings and the writings of the apostles frequently refer to the everlasting nature of His kingdom.

Luke 1:32-33:

"He shall be great, and shall be called the Son of the Highest: and the Lord God shall give unto him the throne of his father David: And he shall reign over the house of Jacob for ever; and of his kingdom there shall be no end."

Key Elements:

- Throne of David: Links Jesus to the Davidic covenant and the promise of an eternal kingdom.

- No End: Emphasizes the eternal nature of Jesus' reign.

Revelation 11:15:

"And the seventh angel sounded; and there were great voices in heaven, saying, The kingdoms of this world are become the kingdoms of our Lord, and of his Christ; and he shall reign for ever and ever."

Key Elements:

- Kingdoms of This World: Indicates the transition of earthly dominions to Christ's rule.

- For Ever and Ever: Reiterates the eternal duration of His reign.

Christ's Role as Judge

Jesus' divine authority includes His role as the eschatological judge, a function that underscores His dominion over all creation.

John 5:22-23:

"For the Father judgeth no man, but hath committed all judgment unto the Son: That all men should honor the Son, even as they honor the Father. He that honoreth not the Son honoreth not the Father which hath sent him."

Key Elements:

- All Judgment: Indicates Jesus' authority to judge humanity.

- Honor the Son: Emphasizes the divine status of Jesus, deserving of the same honor as the Father.

Revelation 20:11-12:

"And I saw a great white throne, and him that sat on it, from whose face the earth and the heaven fled away; and there was found no place for them. And I saw the dead, small and great, stand before God; and the books were opened: and another book was opened, which is the book of life: and the dead were judged out of those things which were written in the books, according to their works."

Key Elements:

- Great White Throne: Symbolizes the ultimate judgment seat of Christ.

- Books Opened: Represents the records of human deeds and the final judgment.

Theological Significance

Divine Authority of Christ

The divine authority of Christ is a central theme in Christian theology, emphasizing His role as the sovereign ruler of all creation.

Biblical References:

- Colossians 1:16-17: "For by him were all things created, that are in heaven, and that are in earth, visible and invisible, whether they be thrones, or dominions, or principalities, or powers: all things were created by him, and for him: And he is before all things, and by him all things consist."

- Hebrews 1:3: "Who being the brightness of his glory, and the express image of his person, and upholding all things by the word of his power, when he had by himself purged our sins, sat down on the right hand of the Majesty on high."

Eternal Dominion

The eternal dominion of Christ assures believers of the unending nature of His reign and the ultimate fulfillment of God's redemptive plan.

Biblical References:

- Daniel 7:14: "And there was given him dominion, and glory, and a kingdom, that all people, nations, and languages, should serve him: his dominion is an everlasting dominion, which shall not pass away, and his kingdom that which shall not be destroyed."

- 1 Peter 5:11: "To him be glory and dominion for ever and ever. Amen."

Eschatological Fulfillment

The eschatological role of Christ as the judge and ruler of the eternal kingdom underscores the future realization of His authority and dominion.

Biblical References:

- Revelation 21:1-4: "And I saw a new heaven and a new earth: for the first heaven and the first earth were passed away; and there was no more sea. And I John saw the holy city, new Jerusalem, coming down from God out of heaven, prepared as a bride adorned for her husband. And I heard a great voice out of heaven saying, Behold, the tabernacle of God is with men, and he will dwell with them, and they shall be his people, and God himself shall be with them, and be their God. And God shall wipe away all tears from their eyes; and there shall be no more death, neither sorrow, nor crying, neither shall there be any more pain: for the former things are passed away."

- Philippians 2:9-11: "Wherefore God also hath highly exalted him, and given him a name which is above every name: That at the name of Jesus every knee should bow, of things in heaven, and things in earth, and things under the earth; And that every tongue should confess that Jesus Christ is Lord, to the glory of God the Father."

Expository Analysis and Strong's Concordance

Using Strong's Concordance, we can delve deeper into the significance of the terms associated with Christ's eternal dominion and divine authority.

Key Terms

- Dominion (שָׁלְטָן, sholtan, Strong's H7985): Represents sovereign authority and control.

- Glory (יְקָר, yeqar, Strong's H3367): Indicates honor, majesty, and splendor.

- Kingdom (מַלְכוּ, malku, Strong's H4437): Represents the realm over which Christ will rule.

Comprehensive Commentary

Daniel 7:13-14:

- The vision of the Son of Man receiving eternal dominion from the Ancient of Days emphasizes the divine origin and authority of Christ's kingdom. This passage sets the foundation for understanding

Jesus' claims to divine authority and eternal dominion.

Matthew 28:18:

- Jesus' declaration of having all authority in heaven and earth underscores the comprehensive nature of His dominion. This authority is not limited to the spiritual realm but extends over all creation.

Revelation 11:15:

- The proclamation that the kingdoms of this world have become the kingdoms of our Lord and His Christ highlights the ultimate fulfillment of God's plan for an eternal kingdom under Christ's rule.

Lessons for Believers

Assurance in Christ's Sovereignty

Believers can find assurance in the knowledge that Christ has ultimate authority over all things. This sovereignty provides comfort and confidence in the face of life's uncertainties.

Hope in the Eternal Kingdom

The promise of an eternal kingdom under Christ's reign offers hope and perspective for believers. This eternal perspective encourages believers to live faithfully and purposefully, knowing that their citizenship is in a kingdom that will never end.

Commitment to Christ's Authority

Recognizing Christ's divine authority calls believers to a deeper commitment to His lordship. This involves submitting to His will, following His teachings, and participating in His mission to advance God's kingdom on earth.

The eternal dominion and divine authority of Christ are foundational truths of the Christian faith. Rooted in the prophetic vision of Daniel 7 and affirmed throughout the New Testament, these themes underscore the comprehensive nature of Christ's rule and the ultimate fulfillment of God's redemptive plan. As we reflect on these truths, may we find assurance in Christ's sovereignty, hope in His eternal kingdom, and a renewed commitment to His authority. The lessons from this chapter continue to resonate, offering timeless truths and hope for believers navigating the complexities of the world.

CHAPTER 05

THE SEVENTY WEEKS PROPHECY

The prophecy of the seventy weeks in Daniel 9 is one of the most intriguing and debated passages in the Bible. This prophecy outlines a timeline of significant events leading to the coming of the Messiah and the fulfillment of God's redemptive plan. In this chapter, we will explore the seventy weeks prophecy, examining its context, interpretation, and theological significance. We will use Bible verses, expository study, and exhaustive Strong's Concordance to provide comprehensive commentary and insights.

The Context of the Seventy Weeks Prophecy

Daniel's Prayer and the Angel Gabriel's Arrival

The prophecy is given in response to Daniel's fervent prayer for his people and the holy city of Jerusalem. Daniel's prayer is recorded in Daniel 9:1-19, where he confesses the sins of Israel and pleads for God's mercy.

Daniel 9:20-23:

"And whiles I was speaking, and praying, and confessing my sin and the sin of my people Israel, and presenting my supplication before the Lord my God for the holy mountain of my God; Yea, whiles I was speaking in prayer, even the man Gabriel, whom I had seen in the vision at the beginning, being caused to fly swiftly, touched me about the time of the evening oblation. And he informed me and talked with me, and said, O Daniel, I am now come forth to give thee skill and understanding. At the beginning of thy supplications, the commandment came forth, and I am come to shew thee; for thou art greatly beloved: therefore understand the matter, and consider the vision."

Key Elements:

- Daniel's Prayer: A heartfelt plea for forgiveness and restoration.

- Gabriel's Arrival: The angel Gabriel is sent to give Daniel understanding and insight into the future.

Strong's Concordance:

- Prayer (תְּפִלָּה, tephillah, Strong's H8605): Indicates intercession and supplication.

- Understanding (בִּינָה, binah, Strong's H998): Refers to insight and discernment.

The Seventy Weeks Prophecy Explained

The Prophecy Delivered

Gabriel's message to Daniel outlines a period of seventy weeks, divided into distinct segments, each with specific events and milestones.

Daniel 9:24-27:

"Seventy weeks are determined upon thy people and upon thy holy city, to finish the transgression, and to make an end of sins, and to make reconciliation for iniquity, and to bring in everlasting righteousness, and to seal up the vision and prophecy, and to anoint the most Holy. Know therefore and understand, that from the going forth of the commandment to restore and to build Jerusalem unto the Messiah the Prince shall be seven weeks, and threescore and two weeks: the street shall be built again, and the wall, even in troublous times. And after threescore and two weeks shall Messiah be cut off, but not for himself: and the people of the prince that shall come shall destroy the city and the sanctuary; and the end thereof shall be with a flood, and unto the end of the war desolations are determined. And he shall confirm the

covenant with many for one week: and in the midst of the week he shall cause the sacrifice and the oblation to cease, and for the overspreading of abominations he shall make it desolate, even until the consummation, and that determined shall be poured upon the desolate."

Key Elements:

- Seventy Weeks: Represents a period of seventy "sevens" (weeks or sets of seven years).

- Messiah the Prince: Refers to the coming of the Anointed One.

- Cut Off: Indicates the death of the Messiah.

- Desolation: Foretells the destruction of the city and sanctuary.

Strong's Concordance:

- Weeks (שָׁבוּעַ, shabuwa, Strong's H7620): Indicates a period of seven, commonly interpreted as years.

- Anoint (מָשַׁח, mashach, Strong's H4886): Refers to consecration or sanctification.

The First Segment: Seven Weeks

The first segment of the seventy weeks is a period of seven weeks (49 years), starting from the command to restore and rebuild Jerusalem.

Biblical Reference:

- Nehemiah 2:1-8: The decree of Artaxerxes to Nehemiah to rebuild Jerusalem marks the beginning of the seventy weeks.

Key Elements:

- Restoration of Jerusalem: The city is rebuilt despite opposition and challenges.

The Second Segment: Sixty-Two Weeks

The second segment is a period of sixty-two weeks (434 years), culminating in the arrival of the Messiah.

Biblical Reference:

- Luke 2:11: The birth of Jesus Christ fulfills the prophecy of the coming Messiah.

Key Elements:

- Arrival of the Messiah: The Anointed One comes to fulfill God's redemptive plan.

The Final Segment: One Week

The final segment is a period of one week (seven years), which includes significant events leading to the end times.

Key Elements:

- Covenant with Many: A covenant is confirmed for one week.

- Cessation of Sacrifice: In the middle of the week, sacrifices cease.

- Abomination and Desolation: Desolation and abominations occur until the consummation.

Interpretation and Theological Significance

The Seventy Weeks as a Prophetic Timeline

The seventy weeks prophecy provides a detailed timeline of significant events in God's redemptive plan, from the restoration of Jerusalem to the end times.

Key Interpretations:

- Historical Fulfillment: Many scholars see the prophecy as being historically fulfilled in the life, death, and resurrection of Jesus Christ.

- Futurist View: Some interpret the final week as a future period of tribulation and the second coming of Christ.

The Role of the Messiah

The prophecy emphasizes the central role of the Messiah in bringing reconciliation for iniquity, ending sin, and establishing everlasting righteousness.

Biblical References:

- Isaiah 53:5-6: "But he was wounded for our transgressions, he was bruised for our iniquities: the chastisement of our peace was upon him; and with his stripes we are healed. All we like sheep have gone astray; we have turned every one to his own way; and the Lord hath laid on him the iniquity of us all."

- Hebrews 9:26: "For then must he often have suffered since the foundation of the world: but now once in the end of the world hath he appeared to put away sin by the sacrifice of himself."

Theological Themes

The prophecy highlights several key theological themes, including God's sovereignty, the fulfillment of prophecy, and the ultimate victory of God's kingdom.

Key Themes:

- God's Sovereignty: The detailed fulfillment of the prophecy demonstrates God's control over history.

- Fulfillment of Prophecy: The prophecy affirms the reliability and accuracy of God's Word.

- Victory of God's Kingdom: The establishment of everlasting righteousness points to the ultimate triumph of God's kingdom.

Expository Analysis and Strong's Concordance

Using Strong's Concordance, we can gain deeper insights into the key terms and concepts in the seventy weeks prophecy.

Key Terms

- Weeks (שָׁבוּעַ, shabuwa, Strong's H7620): Represents a period of seven, commonly interpreted as years.

- Transgression (פֶּשַׁע, pesha, Strong's H6588): Indicates rebellion or sin.

- Reconciliation (כָּפַר, kaphar, Strong's H3722): Refers to atonement or covering.

- Righteousness (צֶדֶק, tsedeq, Strong's H6664): Denotes justice or rightness.

Comprehensive Commentary

Daniel 9:24:

- The purpose of the seventy weeks is outlined: to finish the transgression, end sin, make reconciliation for iniquity, bring in everlasting righteousness, seal up vision and prophecy, and anoint the most Holy. These goals encapsulate the redemptive work of the Messiah.

Daniel 9:25:

- The timeline begins with the decree to restore and rebuild Jerusalem, leading to the arrival of the Messiah. The period of seven weeks plus sixty-two weeks (69 weeks) leads to the Messiah's coming.

Daniel 9:26:

- The Messiah will be "cut off," indicating His sacrificial death. This event brings an end to sin and initiates reconciliation.

Daniel 9:27:

- The final week includes the confirmation of a covenant, the cessation of sacrifices, and the abomination of desolation. This period points to the culmination of God's redemptive plan and the establishment of His kingdom.

Lessons for Believers

Trust in God's Sovereignty

The detailed fulfillment of the seventy-week prophecy encourages believers to trust in God's sovereign control over history and His faithfulness to fulfill His promises.

Assurance of Salvation

The prophecy emphasizes the central role of the Messiah in bringing reconciliation and salvation. Believers can find assurance in the completed work of Christ and the promise of everlasting righteousness.

Hope for the Future

The prophecy points to the ultimate victory of God's kingdom and the establishment of everlasting righteousness. This hope motivates believers to live faithfully and expectantly, looking forward to the fulfillment of God's redemptive plan.

The seventy weeks prophecy in Daniel 9 provides a detailed and profound revelation of God's redemptive plan, centered on the coming of the Messiah and the establishment of His eternal kingdom. This prophecy underscores God's sovereignty, the fulfillment of prophecy, and the ultimate victory of God's kingdom. As we reflect on this prophecy, may we find assurance in God's faithfulness, confidence in the completed work of Christ, and hope in the promise of everlasting righteousness? The lessons from the seventy-week prophecy continue to resonate, offering timeless truths and hope for believers navigating the complexities of the world.

The Timeline Leading to the Anointed One

The prophecy of the seventy weeks in Daniel 9 provides a precise timeline leading to the coming of the Anointed One, the Messiah. This timeline, marked by significant historical events, underscores the accuracy and reliability of biblical prophecy. In this chapter, we will examine the historical details and biblical evidence that validate this prophecy, highlighting key milestones from the decree to rebuild Jerusalem to the arrival of Jesus Christ.

The Starting Point: The Decree to Rebuild Jerusalem

Historical Context

The seventy-week prophecy begins with a decree to restore and rebuild Jerusalem. Historically, this decree can be linked to the Persian king Artaxerxes I, who issued a command that allowed the Jews to return and rebuild their city.

Key Historical Event:

- The Decree of Artaxerxes: In 445 BCE, Artaxerxes I issued a decree to Nehemiah, authorizing him to rebuild Jerusalem's walls and restore the city (Nehemiah 2:1-8).

Biblical Reference:

- Nehemiah 2:1-5: "And it came to pass in the month Nisan, in the twentieth year of Artaxerxes the king, that wine was before him: and I took up the wine, and gave it unto the king. Now I had not been beforetime sad in his presence. Wherefore the king said unto me, Why is thy countenance sad, seeing thou art not sick? this is nothing else but sorrow of heart. Then I was very sore afraid, And said unto the king, Let the king live for ever: why should not my countenance be sad, when the city, the place of my fathers' sepulchres, lieth waste, and the gates thereof are consumed with fire? Then the king said unto me, For what dost thou make request? So I prayed to the God of heaven. And I said unto the king, If it please the king, and if thy servant have found favour in thy sight, that thou wouldest send me unto Judah, unto the city of my fathers' sepulchres, that I may build it."

Significance of the Decree

This decree marks the starting point of the seventy-week prophecy. The timeline begins in 445 BCE, setting the stage for the subsequent periods outlined in Daniel 9:24-27.

The First Segment: Seven Weeks (49 Years)

Restoration of Jerusalem

The first segment of the prophecy spans seven weeks, or 49 years, during which Jerusalem is rebuilt despite considerable opposition and difficulties.

Biblical Reference:

- Nehemiah 6:15-16: "So the wall was finished in the twenty and fifth day of the month Elul, in fifty and two days. And it came to pass, that when all our enemies heard thereof, and all the heathen that were about us saw these things, they were much cast down in their own eyes: for they perceived that this work was wrought of our God."

Historical Evidence

Historical records confirm that the rebuilding of Jerusalem, including its walls and infrastructure, took approximately 49 years, aligning with the prophetic timeline. This period concluded around 396 BCE.

The Second Segment: Sixty-Two Weeks (434 Years)

Leading to the Messiah

The second segment spans sixty-two weeks, or 434 years, following the initial seven weeks. This period leads directly to the arrival of the Messiah, "the Anointed One."

Biblical Reference:

- Daniel 9:25: "Know therefore and understand, that from the going forth of the commandment to restore and to build Jerusalem unto the Messiah the Prince shall be seven weeks, and threescore and two weeks: the street shall be built again, and the wall, even in troublous times."

Historical Evidence

Adding 434 years to the end of the first segment (396 BCE) brings us to approximately 27 CE, a date that coincides with the beginning of Jesus Christ's public ministry. This period saw significant events in Jewish history, including the rule of the Hasmonean dynasty, the Roman conquest of Judea, and the Herodian dynasty's reign.

Key Historical Events:

- Hasmonean Dynasty (167-37 BCE): Established following the Maccabean Revolt, the Hasmonean rulers governed Judea, maintaining relative independence.

- Roman Conquest (63 BCE): Pompey the Great captured Jerusalem, bringing Judea under Roman control.

- Herodian Dynasty (37 BCE - 70 CE): Herod the Great and his successors ruled Judea under Roman oversight, leading to the political context of Jesus' birth and ministry.

The Arrival of the Messiah

Jesus' Public Ministry

The prophetic timeline culminates with the appearance of Jesus Christ, whose ministry began around 27-30 CE. This period aligns with the conclusion of the sixty-two-week segment.

Biblical References:

- Luke 3:1-2, 21-23: "Now in the fifteenth year of the reign of Tiberius Caesar, Pontius Pilate being governor of Judaea, and Herod being tetrarch of Galilee, and his brother Philip tetrarch of Ituraea and of the region of Trachonitis, and Lysanias the tetrarch of Abilene, Annas and Caiaphas being the high priests, the word of God came unto John the son of Zacharias in the wilderness. ... Now when all the people were baptized, it came to pass, that Jesus also being baptized, and praying, the heaven was opened, And the Holy Ghost descended in a bodily shape like a dove upon him, and a voice came from heaven, which said, Thou art my beloved Son; in thee I am well pleased. And Jesus himself began to be about thirty years of age, being (as was supposed) the son of Joseph, which was the son of Heli."

The Cutting Off of the Messiah

The prophecy indicates that after the sixty-two weeks, the Messiah will be "cut off" but not for Himself, pointing to the crucifixion of Jesus.

Biblical Reference:

- Daniel 9:26: "And after threescore and two weeks shall Messiah be cut off, but not for himself: and the people of the prince that shall come shall destroy the city and the sanctuary; and the end thereof shall be with a flood, and unto the end of the war desolations are determined."

New Testament Confirmation:

- Matthew 27:50: "Jesus, when he had cried again with a loud voice, yielded up the ghost."

- John 19:30: "When Jesus therefore had received the vinegar, he said, It is finished: and he bowed his head, and gave up the ghost."

Destruction of Jerusalem

Following the cutting off of the Messiah, the prophecy foretells the destruction of Jerusalem and the sanctuary, which historically occurred in 70 CE when the Romans destroyed the Second Temple.

Historical Event:

- Destruction of Jerusalem (70 CE): Roman legions, led by Titus, besieged and destroyed Jerusalem and the Second Temple, fulfilling the prophetic words.

Biblical Reference:

- Matthew 24:2: "And Jesus said unto them, See ye not all these things? verily I say unto you, There shall not be left here one stone upon another, that shall not be thrown down."

The Final Week: One Week (Seven Years)

The Covenant and the Abomination

The prophecy's final segment describes a one-week period during which a covenant is confirmed, sacrifices cease, and abominations occur, leading to desolation.

Biblical Reference:

- Daniel 9:27: "And he shall confirm the covenant with many for one week: and in the midst of the week he shall cause the sacrifice and the oblation to cease, and for the overspreading of abominations he shall make it desolate, even until the consummation, and that determined shall be poured upon the desolate."

Interpretations of the Final Week

There are varied interpretations regarding the final week, with some viewing it as historically fulfilled in the first century and others seeing it as a future period related to the end times.

Historical View:

- First Century Fulfillment: Some scholars believe the final week refers to events leading up to and including the destruction of Jerusalem in 70 CE.

Futurist View:

- End Times Fulfillment: Others interpret the final week as a future period of tribulation, involving a covenant with a future ruler, cessation of temple sacrifices, and the rise of the Antichrist.

Biblical Reference:

- Matthew 24:15: "When ye therefore shall see the abomination of desolation, spoken of by Daniel the prophet, stand in the holy place, (whoso readeth, let him understand:)"

Theological Significance

Fulfillment of Prophecy

The precise fulfillment of the seventy weeks prophecy underscores the reliability of Scripture and God's sovereign control over history. The detailed timeline leading to the Anointed One highlights God's meticulous orchestration of events to accomplish His redemptive plan.

Biblical References:

- Isaiah 46:10: "Declaring the end from the beginning, and from ancient times the things that are not yet done, saying, My counsel shall stand, and I will do all my pleasure."

- Galatians 4:4: "But when the fulness of the time was come, God sent forth his Son, made of a woman, made under the law."

Assurance of Salvation

The prophecy emphasizes the central role of the Messiah in bringing reconciliation and salvation. Believers can find assurance in the completed work of Christ, who was "cut off" for the sins of humanity.

Biblical References:

- Romans 5:8: "But God commendeth his love toward us, in that, while we were yet sinners, Christ died for us."

- 1 Peter 2:24: "Who his own self bare our sins in his own body on the tree, that we, being dead to sins, should live unto righteousness: by whose stripes ye were healed."

Hope for the Future

The final week of the prophecy points to the culmination of God's redemptive plan and the ultimate victory of His kingdom. Believers are encouraged to live with hope and expectancy, knowing that God's promises will be fulfilled.

Biblical References:

- Revelation 21:1-4: "And I saw a new heaven and a new earth: for the first heaven and the first earth were passed away; and there was no more sea. And I John saw the holy city, new Jerusalem, coming down from God out of heaven, prepared as a bride adorned for her husband. And I heard a great voice out of heaven saying, Behold, the tabernacle of God is with men, and he will dwell with them, and they shall be his people, and God himself shall be with them, and be their God. And God shall wipe away all tears from their eyes;

and there shall be no more death, neither sorrow, nor crying, neither shall there be any more pain: for the former things are passed away."

- 2 Peter 3:13: "Nevertheless we, according to his promise, look for new heavens and a new earth, wherein dwelleth righteousness."

The prophecy of the seventy weeks in Daniel 9 provides a precise and detailed timeline leading to the coming of the Anointed One, Jesus Christ. The historical events and biblical evidence that align with this prophecy underscore its reliability and the sovereign control of God over history. As we reflect on this prophecy, may we find assurance in God's faithfulness, confidence in the completed work of Christ, and hope in the promise of His eternal kingdom. The lessons from the seventy weeks prophecy continue to resonate, offering timeless truths and hope for believers navigating the complexities of the world.

Jesus as the Fulfillment of the Prophecy

The prophecy of the seventy weeks in Daniel 9 is one of the most remarkable and detailed predictions in the Bible, pointing directly to the coming of the Messiah. This prophecy not only foretells the timeline leading to Jesus Christ but also highlights His mission and the significance of His work. In this chapter, we will explore how Jesus fulfills the seventy weeks prophecy, examining the scriptural and historical evidence that supports this fulfillment and the profound theological implications it carries.

The Seventy Weeks Prophecy

The Prophecy Overview

The prophecy of the seventy weeks is delivered by the angel Gabriel to Daniel, outlining a period of seventy "weeks" or sets of seven years, which culminates in the coming of the Messiah.

Daniel 9:24-27:

"Seventy weeks are determined upon thy people and upon thy holy city, to finish the transgression, and to make an end of sins, and to make reconciliation for iniquity, and to bring in everlasting righteousness, and to seal up the vision and prophecy, and to anoint the most Holy. Know therefore and understand, that from the going forth of the commandment to restore and to build Jerusalem unto the Messiah the Prince shall be seven weeks, and threescore and two weeks: the street shall be built again, and the wall, even in troublous times. And after threescore and two weeks shall Messiah be cut off, but not for himself: and the people of the prince that shall come shall destroy the city and the sanctuary; and the end thereof shall be with a flood, and unto the end of the war desolations are determined. And he shall confirm the

covenant with many for one week: and in the midst of the week he shall cause the sacrifice and the oblation to cease, and for the overspreading of abominations he shall make it desolate, even until the consummation, and that determined shall be poured upon the desolate."

Key Elements:

- Seventy Weeks: Represents 490 years.

- Messiah the Prince: Refers to the coming Anointed One.

- Cut Off: Indicates the Messiah's sacrificial death.

- Destruction of the City and Sanctuary: Foretells the destruction of Jerusalem and the Temple.

Strong's Concordance:

- Weeks (שָׁבוּעַ, shabuwa, Strong's H7620): Periods of seven, interpreted as years.

- Anoint (מָשַׁח, mashach, Strong's H4886): To consecrate or sanctify.

Jesus' Fulfillment of the Prophecy

The Timeline to the Messiah

The prophecy's timeline begins with the decree to restore and rebuild Jerusalem, identified with the decree issued by Artaxerxes I in 445 BCE (Nehemiah 2:1-8). This decree marks the start of the seventy weeks.

Historical Context:

- Decree of Artaxerxes (445 BCE): Permission given to Nehemiah to rebuild Jerusalem.

Biblical Reference:

- Nehemiah 2:1-5: "And it came to pass in the month Nisan, in the twentieth year of Artaxerxes the king, that wine was before him: and I took up the wine, and gave it unto the king. Now I had not been beforetime sad in his presence. Wherefore the king said unto me, Why is thy countenance sad, seeing thou art not sick? this is nothing else but sorrow of heart. Then I was very sore afraid, And said unto the king, Let the king live for ever: why should not my countenance be sad, when the city, the place of my fathers' sepulchres, lieth waste, and the gates thereof are consumed with fire? Then the king said unto me, For what dost thou make request? So I prayed to the God of heaven. And I said unto the king, If it please the king, and if thy servant have found favour in thy sight, that thou wouldest send me unto Judah, unto the city of my fathers' sepulchres, that I may build it."

Adding the sixty-nine weeks (7 + 62 weeks = 483 years) to 445 BCE brings us to approximately 27-30 CE, aligning with the start of Jesus' public ministry.

Biblical Reference:

- Luke 3:1-2, 21-23: "Now in the fifteenth year of the reign of Tiberius Caesar, Pontius Pilate being governor of

Judaea, and Herod being tetrarch of Galilee, and his brother Philip tetrarch of Ituraea and of the region of Trachonitis, and Lysanias the tetrarch of Abilene, Annas and Caiaphas being the high priests, the word of God came unto John the son of Zacharias in the wilderness. ... Now when all the people were baptized, it came to pass, that Jesus also being baptized, and praying, the heaven was opened, And the Holy Ghost descended in a bodily shape like a dove upon him, and a voice came from heaven, which said, Thou art my beloved Son; in thee I am well pleased. And Jesus himself began to be about thirty years of age, being (as was supposed) the son of Joseph, which was the son of Heli."

The Messiah Cut Off

The prophecy foretells that after sixty-two weeks, the Messiah will be "cut off," indicating His sacrificial death.

Daniel 9:26:

"And after threescore and two weeks shall Messiah be cut off, but not for himself: and the people of the prince that shall come shall destroy the city and the sanctuary; and the end thereof shall be with a flood, and unto the end of the war desolations are determined."

Fulfillment in Jesus:

- Crucifixion: Jesus was crucified around 30-33 CE, fulfilling the prophecy of being "cut off" for the sins of humanity.

Biblical Reference:

- Matthew 27:50: "Jesus, when he had cried again with a loud voice, yielded up the ghost."

- John 19:30: "When Jesus therefore had received the vinegar, he said, It is finished: and he bowed his head, and gave up the ghost."

The Destruction of Jerusalem

The prophecy also predicts the destruction of the city and the sanctuary, which occurred in 70 CE when the Romans destroyed Jerusalem and the Second Temple.

Historical Event:

- Destruction of Jerusalem (70 CE): Roman legions led by Titus besieged and destroyed Jerusalem, fulfilling the prophecy's prediction of desolation.

Biblical Reference:

- Matthew 24:2: "And Jesus said unto them, See ye not all these things? verily I say unto you, There shall not be left here one stone upon another, that shall not be thrown down."

The Theological Significance of Jesus' Fulfillment

The Messiah's Mission

The prophecy outlines key aspects of the Messiah's mission, all of which Jesus fulfills:

Daniel 9:24:

"Seventy weeks are determined upon thy people and upon thy holy city, to finish the transgression, and to make an end of sins, and to make reconciliation for iniquity, and to bring in everlasting righteousness, and to seal up the vision and prophecy, and to anoint the most Holy."

Fulfillment in Jesus:

- Finish the Transgression: Jesus' death atones for humanity's sins.

- End of Sins: Through His sacrifice, Jesus provides forgiveness and redemption.

- Reconciliation for Iniquity: Jesus reconciles humanity to God.

- Everlasting Righteousness: Jesus' resurrection and reign establish righteousness.

- Seal Up Vision and Prophecy: Jesus' life and work fulfill Old Testament prophecies.

- Anoint the Most Holy: Jesus, the Anointed One, consecrates His followers.

Biblical References:

- Isaiah 53:5-6: "But he was wounded for our transgressions, he was bruised for our iniquities: the chastisement of our peace was upon him; and with his stripes we are healed. All we like sheep have gone astray; we have turned every one to his own way; and the Lord hath laid on him the iniquity of us all."

- Hebrews 9:26: "For then must he often have suffered since the foundation of the world: but now once in the end of the world hath he appeared to put away sin by the sacrifice of himself."

The New Covenant

The prophecy's reference to a covenant being confirmed for one week points to Jesus' establishment of the New Covenant through His death and resurrection.

Daniel 9:27:

"And he shall confirm the covenant with many for one week: and in the midst of the week he shall cause the sacrifice and the oblation to cease, and for the overspreading of abominations he shall make it desolate, even until the consummation, and that determined shall be poured upon the desolate."

Fulfillment in Jesus:

- New Covenant: Jesus' death and resurrection establish a new covenant with humanity, fulfilling and surpassing the old sacrificial system.

Biblical References:

- Luke 22:20: "Likewise also the cup after supper, saying, This cup is the new testament in my blood, which is shed for you."

- Hebrews 8:6: "But now hath he obtained a more excellent ministry, by how much also he is the mediator of a better covenant, which was established upon better promises."

The seventy-week prophecy in Daniel 9 is a remarkable testament to the accuracy and reliability of biblical prophecy, pointing directly to the coming of Jesus Christ. The historical and scriptural evidence overwhelmingly supports Jesus as the fulfillment of this prophecy, highlighting His sacrificial death, the establishment of the New Covenant, and the ultimate redemption He offers.

As we reflect on this prophecy, we gain a deeper understanding of God's sovereign control over history and His meticulous orchestration of events to bring about His redemptive plan. The fulfillment of the seventy-week prophecy in Jesus Christ not only assures us of the reliability of Scripture but also underscores the profound significance of His mission and the hope we have in Him.

May we be encouraged to trust in God's faithfulness, embrace the salvation offered through Jesus, and live with the hope and expectancy of His eternal kingdom. The lessons from the seventy weeks prophecy continue to resonate, offering timeless truths and hope for believers navigating the complexities of the world.

CHAPTER 06

THE ANOINTED ONE CUT-OFF

Daniel 9:26 is a pivotal verse in the prophecy of the seventy weeks, detailing the events surrounding the "cutting off" of the Anointed One, the Messiah. This verse not only predicts the sacrificial death of Jesus Christ but also foretells the subsequent destruction of Jerusalem and the Temple. In this chapter, we will provide a detailed analysis of Daniel 9:26, examining its historical and theological significance, supported by comprehensive Bible references, expository study, and insights from Strong's Concordance.

Daniel 9:26: The Text

Daniel 9:26 (KJV):

"And after threescore and two weeks shall Messiah be cut off, but not for himself: and the people of the prince that shall come shall destroy the city and the sanctuary; and the end thereof shall be with a flood, and unto the end of the war desolations are determined."

Key Elements:

- Threescore and Two Weeks: Represents 62 weeks or 434 years.

- Messiah: The Anointed One, Jesus Christ.

- Cut Off: Indicates the sacrificial death of the Messiah.

- Not for Himself: The Messiah's death is for others, not for His own sins.

- People of the Prince: Refers to the Romans who would destroy Jerusalem.

- Destruction of the City and Sanctuary: Foretells the destruction of Jerusalem and the Temple.

Expository Analysis and Strong's Concordance

Threescore and Two Weeks

Threescore and Two Weeks: This period follows the initial seven weeks (49 years), totaling 69 weeks (483 years) from the decree to rebuild Jerusalem to the coming of the Messiah.

Strong's Concordance:

- Weeks (שָׁבוּעַ, shabuwa, Strong's H7620): Periods of seven, interpreted as years.

Biblical Reference:

- Daniel 9:25: "Know therefore and understand, that from the going forth of the commandment to restore and to build Jerusalem unto the Messiah the Prince shall be seven weeks, and threescore and two weeks: the street shall be built again, and the wall, even in troublous times."

Messiah

Messiah (מָשִׁיחַ, mashiach, Strong's H4899): The Anointed One, referring to Jesus Christ, who is consecrated for a divine purpose.

Biblical References:

- Isaiah 61:1: "The Spirit of the Lord God is upon me; because the Lord hath anointed me to preach good tidings unto the meek; he hath sent me to bind up the brokenhearted, to proclaim liberty to the captives, and the opening of the prison to them that are bound."

- Luke 4:18-21: "The Spirit of the Lord is upon me, because he hath anointed me to preach the gospel to the poor; he hath sent me to heal the brokenhearted, to preach deliverance to the captives, and recovering of sight to the blind, to set at liberty them that are bruised, To preach the acceptable year of the Lord. And he closed the book, and he gave it again to the minister, and sat down. And the eyes of all them that were in the synagogue were fastened on him. And he began to say unto them, This day is this scripture fulfilled in your ears."

Cut Off

Cut Off (כָּרַת, karath, Strong's H3772): Indicates a violent and untimely death. The phrase signifies that the Messiah will be killed.

Biblical References:

- Isaiah 53:8: "He was taken from prison and from judgment: and who shall declare his generation? for he was cut off out of the land of the living: for the transgression of my people was he stricken."

- Matthew 27:50: "Jesus, when he had cried again with a loud voice, yielded up the ghost."

Not for Himself

Not for Himself: This phrase indicates that the Messiah's death is not for His own sins but for the sins of others, underscoring the substitutionary nature of His sacrifice.

Biblical References:

- Isaiah 53:5-6: "But he was wounded for our transgressions, he was bruised for our iniquities: the chastisement of our peace was upon him; and with his stripes we are healed. All we like sheep have gone astray; we have turned every one to his own way; and the Lord hath laid on him the iniquity of us all."

- 2 Corinthians 5:21: "For he hath made him to be sin for us, who knew no sin; that we might be made the righteousness of God in him."

People of the Prince

People of the Prince: Refers to the Roman forces led by Titus, who would come to destroy Jerusalem and the Temple.

Strong's Concordance:

- Prince (נָגִיד, nagid, Strong's H5057): A leader or commander.

Historical Context:

- Destruction of Jerusalem (70 CE): Roman legions under General Titus besieged and destroyed Jerusalem, including the Second Temple.

Biblical References:

- Matthew 24:2: "And Jesus said unto them, See ye not all these things? verily I say unto you, There shall not be left here one stone upon another, that shall not be thrown down."

- Luke 21:20-24: "And when ye shall see Jerusalem compassed with armies, then know that the desolation thereof is nigh. Then let them which are in Judaea flee to the mountains; and let them which are in the midst of it depart out; and let not them that are in the countries enter thereinto. For these be the days of vengeance, that all things which are written may be fulfilled."

Destruction of the City and Sanctuary

Destruction of the City and Sanctuary: This prophecy was fulfilled when the Romans destroyed Jerusalem and the Temple in 70 CE, leading to widespread desolation.

Biblical References:

- Daniel 9:26: "And the people of the prince that shall come shall destroy the city and the sanctuary; and the end thereof shall be with a flood, and unto the end of the war desolations are determined."

- Luke 19:43-44: "For the days shall come upon thee, that thine enemies shall cast a trench about thee, and compass thee round, and keep thee in on every side, And shall lay thee even with the ground, and thy children within thee; and they shall not leave in thee one stone upon another; because thou knewest not the time of thy visitation."

Theological Significance

The Substitutionary Atonement

The phrase "but not for himself" highlights the substitutionary atonement of Jesus Christ. His death was a sacrifice for the sins of humanity, fulfilling the role of the Suffering Servant prophesied in Isaiah 53.

Biblical References:

- John 1:29: "The next day John seeth Jesus coming unto him, and saith, Behold the Lamb of God, which taketh away the sin of the world."

- 1 Peter 2:24: "Who his own self bare our sins in his own body on the tree, that we, being dead to sins, should live unto righteousness: by whose stripes ye were healed."

The Fulfillment of Prophecy

Daniel 9:26 serves as a profound fulfillment of Messianic prophecy, demonstrating the accuracy and reliability of the Scriptures. The precise prediction of the Messiah's death and the subsequent destruction of Jerusalem affirm the divine inspiration of the Bible.

Biblical References:

- Luke 24:44: "And he said unto them, These are the words which I spake unto you, while I was yet with you, that all things must be fulfilled, which were written in the law of Moses, and in the prophets, and in the psalms, concerning me."

- Acts 2:23: "Him, being delivered by the determinate counsel and foreknowledge of God, ye have taken, and by wicked hands have crucified and slain."

The End of the Old Covenant

The destruction of the city and the sanctuary symbolizes the end of the Old Covenant and the establishment of the New Covenant through Jesus Christ. With the cessation of the Temple sacrifices, Jesus' once-for-all sacrifice becomes the central means of atonement.

Biblical References:

- Hebrews 9:12: "Neither by the blood of goats and calves, but by his own blood he entered in once into the holy place, having obtained eternal redemption for us."

- Hebrews 10:10: "By the which will we are sanctified through the offering of the body of Jesus Christ once for all."

Daniel 9:26 is a critical verse in the seventy weeks prophecy, detailing the sacrificial death of the Messiah and the subsequent destruction of Jerusalem. Through comprehensive analysis, we see how this prophecy precisely predicts the timeline and significance of Jesus' crucifixion, underscoring the substitutionary nature of His atonement and the fulfillment of biblical prophecy. The theological implications are profound, highlighting the end of the Old Covenant, the establishment of the New Covenant, and the assurance of salvation through Jesus Christ.

As we reflect on Daniel 9:26, we are reminded of the faithfulness of God in fulfilling

His promises and the central role of Jesus in His redemptive plan. This prophecy continues to offer timeless truths and hope for believers, affirming the reliability of Scripture and the profound significance of the Messiah's mission.

The Crucifixion of Jesus and Its Prophetic Significance

The crucifixion of Jesus Christ stands as the pivotal event in Christian theology, fulfilling numerous Old Testament prophecies and establishing the foundation for the New Covenant. This chapter explores the prophetic significance of Jesus' crucifixion, examining how it fulfills the prophecies in Daniel 9:26 and other scriptural references. We will delve into the historical context, theological implications, and the fulfillment of these prophecies, supported by comprehensive Bible references and expository analysis.

The Prophecy in Daniel 9:26

The Text

Daniel 9:26 (KJV):

"And after threescore and two weeks shall Messiah be cut off, but not for himself: and the people of the prince that shall come shall destroy the city and the sanctuary; and the end thereof shall be with a flood, and unto the end of the war desolations are determined."

Key Elements:

- Threescore and Two Weeks: Represents 62 weeks or 434 years.

- Messiah: The Anointed One, Jesus Christ.

- Cut Off: Indicates the sacrificial death of the Messiah.

- Not for Himself: The Messiah's death is for others, not for His own sins.

- People of the Prince: Refers to the Romans who would destroy Jerusalem.

- Destruction of the City and Sanctuary: Foretells the destruction of Jerusalem and the Temple.

Historical Context

The seventy weeks prophecy given to Daniel by the angel Gabriel outlines a timeline culminating in the coming of the Messiah and His sacrificial death. The decree to rebuild Jerusalem, issued by Artaxerxes I in 445 BCE, marks the beginning of this timeline, leading to the Messiah's arrival and crucifixion.

Biblical Reference:

- Nehemiah 2:1-8: The decree to rebuild Jerusalem issued by Artaxerxes.

The Fulfillment in Jesus' Crucifixion

The Messiah Cut Off

The phrase "shall Messiah be cut off" directly points to the crucifixion of Jesus Christ, an event that is central to the fulfillment of the seventy weeks prophecy.

Biblical References:

- Isaiah 53:8: "He was taken from prison and from judgment: and who shall declare his generation? for he was cut off out of the land of the living: for the transgression of my people was he stricken."

- Matthew 27:50: "Jesus, when he had cried again with a loud voice, yielded up the ghost."

- John 19:30: "When Jesus therefore had received the vinegar, he said, It is finished: and he bowed his head, and gave up the ghost."

The Substitutionary Atonement

The phrase "but not for himself" indicates that the Messiah's death was vicarious, meaning it was for the benefit of others, not for His own sins. This concept is central to the Christian understanding of atonement.

Biblical References:

- Isaiah 53:5-6: "But he was wounded for our transgressions, he was bruised for our iniquities: the chastisement of our peace was upon him; and with his stripes we are healed. All we like sheep have gone astray; we have turned every one to his own way; and the Lord hath laid on him the iniquity of us all."

- 1 Peter 2:24: "Who his own self bare our sins in his own body on the tree, that we, being dead to sins, should live unto righteousness: by whose stripes ye were healed."

- 2 Corinthians 5:21: "For he hath made him to be sin for us, who knew no sin; that we might be made the righteousness of God in him."

The Destruction of Jerusalem

The prophecy also foretells the destruction of the city and the sanctuary, which historically occurred in 70 CE when the Romans destroyed Jerusalem and the Temple. This event underscores the prophetic accuracy of Daniel 9:26.

Historical Event:

- Destruction of Jerusalem (70 CE): Roman legions under General Titus besieged and destroyed Jerusalem, including the Second Temple.

Biblical References:

- Matthew 24:2: "And Jesus said unto them, See ye not all these things? verily I say unto you, There shall not be left here one stone upon another, that shall not be thrown down."

- Luke 19:43-44: "For the days shall come upon thee, that thine enemies shall cast a trench about thee, and compass thee round, and keep thee in on every side, And shall lay thee even with the ground, and thy children within thee; and they shall not leave in thee one stone upon another; because thou knewest not the time of thy visitation."

Theological Significance of the Crucifixion

Fulfillment of Prophecy

Jesus' crucifixion fulfills numerous Old Testament prophecies, demonstrating the reliability and divine inspiration of Scripture.

Biblical References:

- Psalm 22:16-18: "For dogs have compassed me: the assembly of the wicked have inclosed me: they pierced my hands and my feet. I may tell all my bones: they look and stare upon me. They part my garments among them, and cast lots upon my vesture."

- Isaiah 53:3-7: "He is despised and rejected of men; a man of sorrows, and acquainted with grief: and we hid as it were our faces from him; he was despised, and we esteemed him not. Surely he hath borne our griefs, and carried our sorrows: yet we did esteem him stricken, smitten of God, and afflicted. But he was wounded for our transgressions, he was bruised for our iniquities: the chastisement of our peace was upon him; and with his stripes we are healed. All we like sheep have gone astray; we have turned every one to his own way; and the Lord hath laid on him the iniquity of us all. He was oppressed, and he was afflicted, yet he opened not his mouth: he is brought as a lamb to the slaughter, and as a sheep before her shearers is dumb, so he openeth not his mouth."

Substitutionary Atonement

The crucifixion of Jesus is the ultimate act of substitutionary atonement, where He bore the sins of humanity, providing a way for reconciliation with God.

Biblical References:

- Romans 5:8: "But God commendeth his love toward us, in that, while we were yet sinners, Christ died for us."

- Hebrews 9:28: "So Christ was once offered to bear the sins of many; and unto them that look for him shall he appear the second time without sin unto salvation."

The Establishment of the New Covenant

Through His death, Jesus established the New Covenant, which is characterized by the forgiveness of sins and a direct relationship with God.

Biblical References:

- Jeremiah 31:31-34: "Behold, the days come, saith the Lord, that I will make a new covenant with the house of Israel, and with the house of Judah: Not according to the covenant that I made with their fathers in the day that I took them by the hand to bring them out of the land of Egypt; which my covenant they brake, although I was an husband unto them, saith the Lord: But this shall be the covenant that I will make with the house of Israel; After those days, saith the Lord, I will put my law in their inward parts, and write it in their hearts; and will be their God, and they shall be my people. And they shall teach no more every man his neighbour, and every man his brother, saying, Know the Lord: for they shall all know me, from the least of them unto the greatest of them, saith the Lord: for I will forgive their iniquity, and I will remember their sin no more."

- Luke 22:20: "Likewise also the cup after supper, saying, This cup is the new testament in my blood, which is shed for you."

- Hebrews 8:6-13: "But now hath he obtained a more excellent ministry, by how much also he is the mediator of a better covenant, which was established upon better promises. For if that first covenant had been faultless, then should no place have been sought for the second. For finding fault with them, he saith, Behold, the days come, saith the Lord, when I will make a new covenant with the house of Israel and with the house of Judah: Not according to the covenant that I made with their fathers in the day when I took them by the hand to lead them out of the land of Egypt; because they continued not in my covenant, and I regarded them not, saith the Lord. For this is the covenant that I will make with the house of Israel after those days, saith the Lord; I will put my laws into their mind, and write them in their hearts: and I will be to them a God, and they shall be to me a people: And they shall not teach every man his neighbour, and every man his brother, saying, Know the Lord: for all shall know me, from the least to the greatest. For I will be merciful to their unrighteousness, and their sins and their iniquities will I remember no more. In that he saith, A new covenant, he hath made the first old. Now that which decayeth and waxeth old is ready to vanish away."

The Victory Over Sin and Death

The crucifixion and subsequent resurrection of Jesus signify His victory over sin and death, providing eternal life to all who believe in Him.

Biblical References:

- 1 Corinthians 15:3-4: "For I delivered unto you first of all that which I also received, how that Christ died for our sins according to the scriptures; And that he was buried, and that he rose again the third day according to the scriptures."

- Romans 6:9-10: "Knowing that Christ being raised from the dead dieth no more; death hath no more dominion over him. For in that he died, he died unto sin once: but in that he liveth, he liveth unto God."

- 1 Peter 1:3-4: "Blessed be the God and Father of our Lord Jesus Christ, which according to his abundant mercy hath begotten us again unto a lively hope by the resurrection of Jesus Christ from the dead, To an inheritance incorruptible, and undefiled, and that fadeth not away, reserved in heaven for you."

The crucifixion of Jesus Christ is the fulfillment of the prophecy in Daniel 9:26 and numerous other Old Testament predictions. This event stands at the heart of the Christian faith, demonstrating the reliability of Scripture, the depth of God's love, and the profound significance of Jesus' atoning sacrifice. Through His death, Jesus fulfills the role of the Suffering Servant, establishes the New Covenant, and provides victory over sin and death.

As we reflect on the crucifixion and its prophetic significance, we are reminded of the faithfulness of God in fulfilling His promises and the central role of Jesus in His redemptive plan. This understanding encourages us to trust in God's sovereignty, embrace the salvation offered through Jesus, and live with the hope and expectancy of His eternal kingdom. The lessons from the crucifixion continue to resonate, offering timeless truths and hope for believers navigating the complexities of the world.

The New Covenant Established Through Christ

The New Covenant, established through the sacrificial death and resurrection of Jesus Christ, represents a foundational shift in the relationship between God and humanity. This covenant, foretold by the prophets and fulfilled in the New Testament, brings about forgiveness of sins, a new heart, and a direct relationship with God. In this chapter, we will explore the biblical foundations, theological significance, and implications of the New Covenant, supported by comprehensive Bible references and expository analysis.

The Promise of the New Covenant

Old Testament Prophecies

The concept of a New Covenant is rooted in the Old Testament, where prophets like Jeremiah and Ezekiel foretold a future covenant that would surpass the Old Covenant given through Moses.

Jeremiah 31:31-34:

"Behold, the days come, saith the Lord, that I will make a new covenant with the house of Israel, and with the house of Judah: Not according to the covenant that I made with their fathers in the day that I took them by the hand to bring them out of the land of Egypt; which my covenant they brake, although I was an husband unto them, saith the Lord: But this shall be the covenant that I will make with the house of Israel; After those days, saith the Lord, I will put my law in their inward parts, and write it in their hearts; and will be their God, and they shall be my people. And they shall teach no more every man his neighbour, and every man his brother, saying, Know the Lord: for they shall all know me, from the least of them unto the greatest of them, saith the Lord: for I will forgive their iniquity, and I will remember their sin no more."

Ezekiel 36:26-27:

"A new heart also will I give you, and a new spirit will I put within you: and I will take away the stony heart out of your flesh, and I will give you an heart of flesh. And I will put my spirit within you, and cause you to walk in my statutes, and ye shall keep my judgments, and do them."

Key Elements:

- New Covenant: A future, transformative agreement between God and His people.

- Internal Law: God's laws written on the hearts of believers.

- Forgiveness of Sins: Complete forgiveness and removal of sin.

- New Heart and Spirit: Transformation of the inner person through the Holy Spirit.

The Old Covenant's Limitations

The Old Covenant, given through Moses, involved the Law and sacrifices, which could not fully remove sin or change the human heart.

Hebrews 8:7-9:

"For if that first covenant had been faultless, then should no place have been sought for the second. For finding fault with them, he saith, Behold, the days come, saith the Lord, when I will make a new covenant with the house of Israel and with the house of Judah: Not according to the covenant that I made with their fathers in the day when I took them by the hand to lead them out of the land of Egypt; because they continued not in my covenant, and I regarded them not, saith the Lord."

Key Elements:

- Faults of the Old Covenant: The inability to perfect those who followed it.

- Need for a New Covenant: A better covenant based on better promises.

The Establishment of the New Covenant

Jesus' Role in the New Covenant

Jesus Christ, through His life, death, and resurrection, established the New Covenant. His sacrifice on the cross serves as the foundation of this covenant.

Luke 22:20:

"Likewise also the cup after supper, saying, This cup is the new testament in my blood, which is shed for you."

Matthew 26:28:

"For this is my blood of the new testament, which is shed for many for the remission of sins."

Key Elements:

- Jesus' Blood: The basis of the New Covenant, symbolizing His sacrificial death.

- Remission of Sins: Forgiveness and cleansing from sin through Jesus' sacrifice.

Strong's Concordance:

- New (καινός, kainos, Strong's G2537): Fresh, unused, novel.

- Covenant (διαθήκη, diathēkē, Strong's G1242): A testament or agreement, often a solemn contract.

The Sacrificial System Fulfilled

Jesus' sacrifice fulfilled the requirements of the Old Covenant sacrifices, offering a once-for-all atonement for sin.

Hebrews 9:12-15:

"Neither by the blood of goats and calves, but by his own blood he entered in once into the holy place, having obtained eternal redemption for us. For if the blood of bulls and of goats, and the ashes of an heifer sprinkling the unclean, sanctifieth to the purifying of the flesh: How much more shall the blood of Christ, who through the eternal Spirit offered himself without spot to God, purge your conscience from dead works to serve the living God? And for this cause he is the mediator of the new testament, that by means of death, for the redemption of the transgressions that were under the first testament, they which are called might receive the promise of eternal inheritance."

Key Elements:

- Eternal Redemption: Achieved through Jesus' once-for-all sacrifice.

- Mediator of the New Covenant: Jesus as the intermediary who establishes the New Covenant.

- Cleansing Conscience: The internal transformation that allows believers to serve God.

The Resurrection and Ascension

The resurrection and ascension of Jesus confirm His authority and the efficacy of the New Covenant, ensuring that He intercedes for believers.

Hebrews 7:24-25:

"But this man, because he continueth ever, hath an unchangeable priesthood. Wherefore he is able also to save them to the uttermost that come unto God by him, seeing he ever liveth to make intercession for them."

Romans 8:34:

"Who is he that condemneth? It is Christ that died, yea rather, that is risen again, who is even at the right hand of God, who also maketh intercession for us."

Key Elements:

- Unchangeable Priesthood: Jesus' eternal role as High Priest.

- Intercession: Jesus' ongoing role in advocating for believers.

Theological Significance of the New Covenant

Forgiveness of Sins

The New Covenant provides complete forgiveness of sins, a central promise fulfilled through Jesus' atonement.

Biblical References:

- Ephesians 1:7: "In whom we have redemption through his blood, the forgiveness of sins, according to the riches of his grace."

- Hebrews 10:17-18: "And their sins and iniquities will I remember no more. Now where remission of these is, there is no more offering for sin."

A New Heart and Spirit

The New Covenant promises a transformed heart and the indwelling of the Holy Spirit, enabling believers to live according to God's will.

Biblical References:

- 2 Corinthians 5:17: "Therefore if any man be in Christ, he is a new creature: old things are passed away; behold, all things are become new."

- Galatians 5:22-23: "But the fruit of the Spirit is love, joy, peace, longsuffering, gentleness, goodness, faith, Meekness, temperance: against such there is no law."

Direct Relationship with God

Under the New Covenant, believers have direct access to God, eliminating the need for a human intermediary.

Biblical References:

- Hebrews 4:16: "Let us therefore come boldly unto the throne of grace, that we may obtain mercy, and find grace to help in time of need."

- John 14:6: "Jesus saith unto him, I am the way, the truth, and the life: no man cometh unto the Father, but by me."

The Law Written on Hearts

The New Covenant internalizes God's law, making it a matter of the heart rather than external adherence.

Biblical References:

- Romans 8:2-4: "For the law of the Spirit of life in Christ Jesus hath made me free from the law of sin and death. For what the law could not do, in that it was weak through the flesh, God sending his own Son in the likeness of sinful flesh, and for sin, condemned sin in the flesh: That the righteousness of the law might be fulfilled in us, who walk not after the flesh, but after the Spirit."

- Hebrews 8:10: "For this is the covenant that I will make with the house of Israel after those days, saith the Lord; I will put my laws into their mind, and write them in their hearts: and I will be to them a God, and they shall be to me a people."

Implications of the New Covenant for Believers

Assurance of Salvation

Believers can have confidence in their salvation, knowing that it is secured by Jesus' perfect sacrifice and His ongoing intercession.

Biblical References:

- John 10:28-29: "And I give unto them eternal life; and they shall never perish, neither shall any man pluck them out of my hand. My Father, which gave them me, is greater than all; and no man is able to pluck them out of my Father's hand."

- Romans 8:38-39: "For I am persuaded, that neither death, nor life, nor angels, nor principalities, nor powers, nor things present, nor things to come, Nor height, nor depth, nor any other creature, shall be able to separate us from the love of God, which is in Christ Jesus our Lord."

Empowerment by the Holy Spirit

Believers are empowered by the Holy Spirit to live godly lives, reflecting the character of Christ and fulfilling God's purposes.

Biblical References:

- Acts 1:8: "But ye shall receive power, after that the Holy Ghost is come upon you: and ye shall be witnesses unto me both in Jerusalem, and in all Judaea, and in Samaria, and unto the uttermost part of the earth."

- Galatians 5:16: "This I say then, Walk in the Spirit, and ye shall not fulfil the lust of the flesh."

A Life of Transformation

The New Covenant calls believers to a life of continual transformation, growing in holiness and reflecting God's love.

Biblical References:

- Romans 12:1-2: "I beseech you therefore, brethren, by the mercies of God, that ye present your bodies a living sacrifice, holy, acceptable unto God, which is your reasonable service. And be not conformed to this world: but be ye transformed by the renewing of your mind, that ye may prove what is that good, and acceptable, and perfect, will of God."

- Philippians 1:6: "Being confident of this very thing, that he which hath begun a good work in you will perform it until the day of Jesus Christ."

The New Covenant established through Jesus Christ marks a transformative era in God's relationship with humanity. This covenant, prophesied in the Old Testament and fulfilled in the New, brings forgiveness of sins, a new heart, the indwelling of the Holy Spirit, and a direct relationship with God. As believers, we are called to live in the assurance of our salvation, empowered by the Holy Spirit, and continually transformed by God's grace.

Reflecting on the New Covenant, we see the fulfillment of God's promises and the depth of His love for humanity. This covenant underscores the centrality of Jesus' sacrifice and resurrection, offering timeless truths and hope for believers navigating the complexities of the world. May we embrace the fullness of the New Covenant, living lives that honor God and reflect His love to those around us.

CHAPTER 07

LESSONS FROM THE LIFE OF JESUS

The life and teachings of Jesus Christ offer profound lessons that are not only central to the Christian faith but also provide practical guidance for daily living. Jesus' teachings encompass love, forgiveness, humility, faith, and service, among other virtues. In this chapter, we will explore some of the key teachings of Jesus and their practical applications, highlighting how these lessons can transform our lives and relationships.

The Greatest Commandments

Love for God and Neighbor

Jesus summarized the essence of the Law with the commandments to love God and love one's neighbor, emphasizing that these are the foundation of all other commandments.

Matthew 22:37-40:

"Jesus said unto him, Thou shalt love the Lord thy God with all thy heart, and with all thy soul, and with all thy mind. This is the first and great commandment. And the second is like unto it, Thou shalt love thy neighbour as thyself. On these two commandments hang all the law and the prophets."

Key Elements:

- Love for God: A wholehearted devotion to God.

- Love for Neighbor: Treating others with the same care and respect as oneself.

Practical Applications:

- Daily Devotion: Setting aside time each day for prayer, worship, and reading Scripture to deepen one's relationship with God.

- Acts of Kindness: Showing kindness, compassion, and generosity to others, especially those in need.

The Sermon on the Mount

The Beatitudes

The Beatitudes, part of the Sermon on the Mount, describe the attitudes and behaviors that characterize the citizens of God's kingdom.

Matthew 5:3-12:

"Blessed are the poor in spirit: for theirs is the kingdom of heaven. Blessed are they that mourn: for they shall be comforted. Blessed are the meek: for they shall inherit the earth. Blessed are they which do hunger and thirst after righteousness: for they shall be filled. Blessed are the merciful: for they shall obtain mercy. Blessed are the pure in heart: for they shall see God. Blessed are the peacemakers: for they shall be called the children of God. Blessed are they which are persecuted for righteousness' sake: for theirs is the kingdom of heaven. Blessed are ye when men shall revile you, and persecute you, and shall say all manner of evil against you falsely, for my sake. Rejoice, and be exceeding glad: for great is your reward in heaven: for so persecuted they the prophets which were before you."

Key Elements:

- Poor in Spirit: Humility and dependence on God.

- Mourn: Sorrow for sin and suffering.

- Meek: Gentleness and self-control.

- Hunger and Thirst for Righteousness: A deep desire for justice and holiness.

- Merciful: Compassionate and forgiving.

- Pure in Heart: Sincerity and moral integrity.

- Peacemakers: Promoting peace and reconciliation.

- Persecuted for Righteousness: Enduring suffering for doing what is right.

Practical Applications:

- Humility: Acknowledging our dependence on God and treating others with respect.

- Compassion: Comforting those who are suffering and showing mercy to others.

- Pursuing Righteousness: Striving for justice and holiness in our personal and communal lives.

- Peacemaking: Working towards resolving conflicts and promoting harmony.

Salt and Light

Jesus called His followers to be the salt of the earth and the light of the world, influencing society positively and reflecting God's truth.

Matthew 5:13-16:

"Ye are the salt of the earth: but if the salt have lost his savour, wherewith shall it be salted? it is thenceforth good for nothing, but to be cast out, and to be trodden under foot of men. Ye are the light of the world. A city that is set on a hill cannot be hid. Neither do men light a candle, and put it under a bushel, but on a candlestick; and it giveth light unto all that are in the house. Let your light so shine before men, that they may see your good works, and glorify your Father which is in heaven."

Key Elements:

- Salt of the Earth: Preserving goodness and adding flavor to life.

- Light of the World: Illuminating truth and goodness in a dark world.

Practical Applications:

- Positive Influence: Living in a way that positively impacts others and reflects God's love.

- Witnessing: Sharing the gospel through words and actions.

Parables of Jesus

The Good Samaritan

The parable of the Good Samaritan teaches the importance of showing mercy and compassion to others, regardless of social or ethnic boundaries.

Luke 10:30-37:

"And Jesus answering said, A certain man went down from Jerusalem to Jericho, and fell among thieves, which stripped him of his raiment, and wounded him, and departed, leaving him half dead. And by chance there came down a certain priest that way: and when he saw him, he passed by on the other side. And likewise a Levite, when he was at the place, came and looked on him, and passed by on the other side. But a certain Samaritan, as he journeyed, came where he was: and when he saw him, he had compassion on him, And went to him, and bound up his wounds, pouring in oil and wine, and set him on his own beast, and brought him to an inn, and took care of him. And on the morrow when he departed, he took out two pence, and gave them to the host, and said unto him, Take care of him; and whatsoever thou spendest more, when I come again, I will repay thee. Which now of these three, thinkest thou, was neighbour unto him that fell among the thieves? And he said, He that shewed mercy on him. Then said Jesus unto him, Go, and do thou likewise."

Key Elements:

- Compassion: Acting out of love and care for others.

- Neighbor: Anyone in need, regardless of background.

Practical Applications:

- Helping Others: Offering assistance and support to those in need, regardless of their social status or ethnicity.

- Mercy: Extending grace and kindness to everyone we encounter.

The Prodigal Son

The parable of the Prodigal Son illustrates God's unconditional love and forgiveness for those who repent and return to Him.

Luke 15:11-24:

"And he said, A certain man had two sons: And the younger of them said to his father, Father, give me the portion of goods that falleth to me. And he divided unto them his living. And not many days after the younger son gathered all together, and took his journey into a far country, and there wasted his substance with riotous living. And when he had spent all, there arose a mighty famine in that land; and he began to be in want. And he went and joined himself to a citizen of that country; and he sent him into his fields to feed swine. And he would fain have filled his belly with the husks that the swine did eat: and no man gave unto him. And when he came to himself, he said, How many hired servants of my father's have bread enough and to spare, and I perish with hunger! I will arise and go to my father, and will say unto him, Father, I have sinned against heaven, and before thee, And am no more worthy to be called thy son: make me as one of thy hired servants. And he arose, and came to his father. But when he was yet a great way off, his father saw him, and had compassion, and ran, and fell on his neck, and kissed him. And the son said unto him, Father, I have sinned against heaven, and in thy sight, and am no more worthy to be called thy son. But the father said to his servants, Bring forth the best robe, and put it on him; and put a ring on his hand, and shoes on his feet: And bring hither the fatted calf, and kill it; and let us eat, and be merry: For this my son was dead, and is alive again; he was lost, and is found. And they began to be merry."

Key Elements:

- Repentance: Recognizing one's sins and turning back to God.

- Forgiveness: God's readiness to forgive and restore those who repent.

Practical Applications:

- Repentance: Regularly examining our lives and seeking God's forgiveness for our sins.

- Forgiveness: Extending forgiveness to others, reflecting God's grace.

Jesus' Teachings on Prayer

The Lord's Prayer

Jesus taught His disciples how to pray, providing a model that emphasizes worship, dependence on God, and seeking His will.

Matthew 6:9-13:

"After this manner therefore pray ye: Our Father which art in heaven, Hallowed be thy name. Thy kingdom come, Thy will be done in earth, as it is in heaven. Give us this day our daily bread. And forgive us our debts, as we forgive our debtors. And lead us not into temptation, but deliver us from evil: For thine is the kingdom, and the power, and the glory, for ever. Amen."

Key Elements:

- Worship: Honoring God's name.

- Dependence: Asking for daily needs.

- Forgiveness: Seeking and extending forgiveness.

- Guidance: Asking for protection from temptation and evil.

Practical Applications:

- Regular Prayer: Making prayer a daily habit, following the model Jesus provided.

- Dependence on God: Trusting God for our daily needs and guidance.

Persistent Prayer

Jesus encouraged His followers to be persistent in prayer, trusting that God hears and responds to their requests.

Luke 18:1-8:

"And he spake a parable unto them to this end, that men ought always to pray, and not to faint; Saying, There was in a city a judge, which feared not God, neither regarded man: And there was a widow in that city; and she came unto him, saying, Avenge me of mine adversary. And he would not for a while: but afterward he said within himself, Though I fear not God, nor regard man; Yet because this widow troubleth me, I will avenge her, lest by her continual coming she weary me. And the Lord said, Hear what the unjust judge saith. And shall not God avenge his own elect, which cry day and night unto him, though he bear long with them? I tell you that he will avenge them speedily. Nevertheless when the Son of man cometh, shall he find faith on the earth?"

Key Elements:

- Persistence: Continuously bringing our needs before God.

- Faith: Trusting in God's justice and timing.

Practical Applications:

- Consistent Prayer: Maintaining a consistent and persistent prayer life.

- Trust in God: Believing in God's timing and justice, even when answers are delayed.

Jesus' Teachings on Forgiveness

Unlimited Forgiveness

Jesus taught that forgiveness should be limitless, reflecting the boundless forgiveness we receive from God.

Matthew 18:21-22:

"Then came Peter to him, and said, Lord, how oft shall my brother sin against me, and I forgive him? till seven times? Jesus saith unto him, I say not unto thee, Until seven times: but, Until seventy times seven."

Key Elements:

- Limitless Forgiveness: Forgiving others repeatedly without keeping count.

Practical Applications:

- Forgiving Others: Practicing forgiveness in our daily interactions, refusing to hold grudges.

Parable of the Unforgiving Servant

Jesus illustrated the importance of forgiveness through the parable of the unforgiving servant, emphasizing the need to forgive as we have been forgiven.

Matthew 18:23-35:

"Therefore is the kingdom of heaven likened unto a certain king, which would take account of his servants. And when he had begun to reckon, one was brought unto him, which owed him ten thousand talents. But forasmuch as he had not to pay, his lord commanded him to be sold, and his wife, and children, and all that he had, and payment to be made. The servant therefore fell down, and worshipped him, saying, Lord, have patience with me, and I will pay thee all.

Then the lord of that servant was moved with compassion, and loosed him, and forgave him the debt. But the same servant went out, and found one of his fellowservants, which owed him an hundred pence: and he laid hands on him, and took him by the throat, saying, Pay me that thou owest. And his fellowservant fell down at his feet, and besought him, saying, Have patience with me, and I will pay thee all. And he would not: but went and cast him into prison, till he should pay the debt. So when his fellowservants saw what was done, they were very sorry, and came and told unto their lord all that was done. Then his lord, after that he had called him, said unto him, O thou wicked servant, I forgave thee all that debt, because thou desiredst me: Shouldest not thou also have had compassion on thy fellowservant, even as I had pity on thee? And his lord was wroth, and delivered him to the tormentors, till he should pay all that was due unto him. So likewise shall my heavenly Father do also unto you, if ye from your hearts forgive not every one his brother their trespasses."

Key Elements:

- Compassion: Showing the same compassion and forgiveness we have received from God.

- Consequences of Unforgiveness: The importance of forgiving others to avoid God's judgment.

Practical Applications:

- Forgiving from the Heart: Truly forgiving others, not just outwardly but from the heart.

- Reflecting God's Forgiveness: Extending the grace we have received to others.

The teachings of Jesus Christ offer timeless lessons that are deeply relevant for our daily lives. From loving God and our neighbors to embodying humility, compassion, forgiveness, and faith, Jesus' instructions provide a blueprint for living a life that honors God and serves others.

As we reflect on these teachings, we are called to apply them in practical ways, transforming our relationships, our communities, and ourselves. By following the example of Jesus, we can become salt and light in the world, demonstrating the love and truth of God in everything we do. The lessons from the life of Jesus continue to resonate, offering guidance, hope, and inspiration for believers navigating the complexities of the world.

Parables, Miracles, and the Sermon on the Mount

The teachings and actions of Jesus Christ provide a profound foundation for Christian faith and practice. Among His most influential methods were parables, miracles, and the Sermon on the Mount. Each of these components illustrates key aspects of the kingdom of God and offers practical lessons for daily living. In this chapter, we will explore the significance of Jesus' parables, His miracles, and the Sermon on the Mount, and discuss their practical applications for believers today.

Parables of Jesus

The Purpose of Parables

Jesus often used parables to teach profound truths in simple, relatable stories. Parables reveal the mysteries of the kingdom of God to those with receptive hearts while concealing them from the hard-hearted.

Matthew 13:10-11:

"And the disciples came, and said unto him, Why speakest thou unto them in parables? He answered and said unto them, Because it is given unto you to know the mysteries of the kingdom of heaven, but to them it is not given."

Key Elements:

- Revelation: Parables reveal divine truths to those open to understanding.

- Concealment: They hide truths from those who are not receptive.

Practical Applications:

- Seeking Understanding: Approaching Jesus' teachings with a humble and open heart, seeking to understand their deeper meanings.

- Reflecting on Stories: Meditating on the parables and their implications for our lives.

The Parable of the Sower

The Parable of the Sower highlights different responses to the message of the kingdom, illustrating how the condition of one's heart affects their receptivity to God's word.

Matthew 13:3-9:

"And he spake many things unto them in parables, saying, Behold, a sower went forth to sow; And when he sowed, some seeds fell by the way side, and the fowls came and devoured them up: Some fell upon stony places, where they had not much earth: and forthwith they sprung up, because they had no deepness of earth: And when the sun was up, they were scorched; and because they had no root, they withered away. And some fell among thorns; and the thorns sprung up, and choked them: But other fell into good ground, and brought forth fruit, some an hundredfold, some sixtyfold, some thirtyfold. Who hath ears to hear, let him hear."

Key Elements:

- Wayside: Represents those who hear the word but do not understand it, and it is quickly taken away.

- Stony Places: Those who receive the word with joy but fall away when trouble arises.

- Thorns: Those who hear the word but are choked by life's worries and wealth.

- Good Ground: Those who hear, understand, and produce a fruitful harvest.

Practical Applications:

- Cultivating a Receptive Heart: Preparing our hearts to receive and retain God's word.

- Overcoming Distractions: Avoiding the cares and distractions that can choke out spiritual growth.

The Parable of the Good Samaritan

This parable teaches about love and mercy, illustrating the call to love and serve our neighbors regardless of their background.

Luke 10:30-37:

"And Jesus answering said, A certain man went down from Jerusalem to Jericho, and fell among thieves, which stripped him of his raiment, and wounded him, and departed, leaving him half dead. And by chance there came down a certain priest that way: and when he saw him, he passed by on the other side. And likewise a Levite, when he was at the place, came and looked on him, and passed by on the other side. But a certain Samaritan, as he journeyed, came where he was: and when he saw him, he had compassion on him, And went to him, and bound up his wounds, pouring in oil and wine, and set him on his own beast, and brought him to an inn, and took care of him. And on the morrow when he departed, he took out two pence, and gave them to the host, and said unto him, Take care of him; and whatsoever thou spendest more, when I come again, I will repay thee. Which now of these three, thinkest thou, was neighbour unto him that fell among the thieves? And he said, He that shewed mercy on him. Then said Jesus unto him, Go, and do thou likewise."

Key Elements:

- Compassion: Demonstrating love and mercy to others.

- Neighbor: Redefining neighbor as anyone in need.

Practical Applications:

- Showing Mercy: Actively seeking to help those in need, regardless of their background.

- Loving Unconditionally: Embracing the call to love and serve all people.

Miracles of Jesus

The Purpose of Miracles

Jesus' miracles served to demonstrate His divine authority, reveal His compassion, and provide signs of the kingdom of God.

John 20:30-31:

"And many other signs truly did Jesus in the presence of his disciples, which are not written in this book: But these are written, that ye might believe that Jesus is the Christ, the Son of God; and that believing ye might have life through his name."

Key Elements:

- Divine Authority: Miracles authenticate Jesus' identity as the Son of God.

- Compassion: Miracles reveal Jesus' deep compassion for humanity.

- Signs of the Kingdom: They point to the reality of God's kingdom breaking into the world.

Practical Applications:

- Faith in Jesus: Strengthening our faith in Jesus as the Son of God.

- Emulating Compassion: Being moved by compassion to help those in need.

The Feeding of the 5,000

The miracle of feeding the 5,000 illustrates Jesus' provision and power, as well as His compassion for the hungry.

Matthew 14:15-21:

"And when it was evening, his disciples came to him, saying, This is a desert place, and the time is now past; send the multitude away, that they may go into the villages, and buy themselves victuals. But Jesus said unto them, They need not depart; give ye them to eat. And they say unto him, We have here but five loaves, and two fishes. He said, Bring them hither to me. And he commanded the multitude to sit down on the grass, and took the five loaves, and the two fishes, and looking up to heaven, he blessed, and brake, and gave the loaves to his disciples, and the disciples to the multitude. And they did all eat, and were filled: and they took up of the fragments that remained twelve baskets full. And they that had eaten were about five thousand men, beside women and children."

Key Elements:

- Provision: Jesus meets the physical needs of the people.

- Power: Demonstrates Jesus' divine power to multiply resources.

- Compassion: Reflects Jesus' care for the well-being of the crowd.

Practical Applications:

- Trusting in God's Provision: Relying on God to meet our needs.

- Generosity: Sharing our resources with others, trusting in God's ability to multiply our efforts.

Healing the Blind Man

Jesus' healing of the blind man highlights His power to bring both physical and spiritual sight, demonstrating His role as the Light of the World.

John 9:1-7:

"And as Jesus passed by, he saw a man which was blind from his birth. And his disciples asked him, saying, Master, who did sin, this man, or his parents, that he was born blind? Jesus answered, Neither hath this man sinned, nor his parents: but that the works of God should be made manifest in him. I must work the works of him that sent me, while it is day: the night cometh, when no man can work. As long as I am in the world, I am the light of the world. When he had thus spoken, he spat on the ground, and made clay of the spittle, and he anointed the eyes of the blind man with the clay, And said unto him, Go, wash in the pool of Siloam, (which is by interpretation, Sent.) He went his way therefore, and washed, and came seeing."

Key Elements:

- Physical Healing: Restoring sight to the blind man.

- Spiritual Insight: Revealing Jesus as the Light of the World.

- Glory to God: Demonstrating God's power and purpose.

Practical Applications:

- Seeking Spiritual Insight: Asking God to open our spiritual eyes to His truth.

- Reflecting Light: Being a light to others by sharing the gospel and living out our faith.

The Sermon on the Mount

The Beatitudes

The Beatitudes outline the characteristics of those who are blessed in God's kingdom, emphasizing inner virtues and attitudes.

Matthew 5:3-12:

"Blessed are the poor in spirit: for theirs is the kingdom of heaven. Blessed are they that mourn: for they shall be comforted. Blessed are the meek: for they shall inherit the earth. Blessed are they which do hunger and thirst after righteousness: for they shall be filled. Blessed are the merciful: for they shall obtain mercy. Blessed are the pure in heart: for they shall see God. Blessed are the peacemakers: for they shall be called the children of God. Blessed are they which are persecuted for righteousness' sake: for theirs is the kingdom of heaven. Blessed are ye when men shall revile you, and persecute you, and shall say all manner of evil against you falsely, for my sake. Rejoice, and be exceeding glad: for great is your reward in heaven: for so persecuted they the prophets which were before you."

Key Elements:

- Poor in Spirit: Humility and dependence on God.

- Mourn: Sorrow for sin and suffering.

- Meek: Gentleness and self-control.

- Hunger and Thirst for Righteousness: A deep desire for justice and holiness.

- Merciful: Compassionate and forgiving.

- Pure in Heart: Sincerity and moral integrity.

- Peacemakers: Promoting peace and reconciliation.

- Persecuted for Righteousness: Enduring suffering for doing what is right.

Practical Applications:

- Humility: Acknowledging our dependence on God and treating others with respect.

- Compassion: Comforting those who are suffering and showing mercy to others.

- Pursuing Righteousness: Striving for justice and holiness in our personal and communal lives.

- Peacemaking: Working towards resolving conflicts and promoting harmony.

Salt and Light

Jesus called His followers to be the salt of the earth and the light of the world, influencing society positively and reflecting God's truth.

Matthew 5:13-16:

"Ye are the salt of the earth: but if the salt have lost his savour, wherewith shall it be salted? it is thenceforth good for nothing, but to be cast out, and to be trodden under foot of men. Ye are the light of the world. A city that is set on a hill cannot be hid. Neither do men light a candle, and put it under a bushel, but on a candlestick; and it giveth light unto all that are in the house. Let your light so shine before men, that they may see your good works, and glorify your Father which is in heaven."

Key Elements:

- Salt of the Earth: Preserving goodness and adding flavor to life.

- Light of the World: Illuminating truth and goodness in a dark world.

Practical Applications:

- Positive Influence: Living in a way that positively impacts others and reflects God's love.

- Witnessing: Sharing the gospel through words and actions.

The Lord's Prayer

Jesus taught His disciples how to pray, providing a model that emphasizes worship, dependence on God, and seeking His will.

Matthew 6:9-13:

"After this manner therefore pray ye: Our Father which art in heaven, Hallowed be thy name. Thy kingdom come, Thy will be done in earth, as it is in heaven. Give us this day our daily bread. And forgive us our debts, as we forgive our debtors. And lead us not into temptation, but deliver us from evil: For thine is the kingdom, and the power, and the glory, for ever. Amen."

Key Elements:

- Worship: Honoring God's name.

- Dependence: Asking for daily needs.

- Forgiveness: Seeking and extending forgiveness.

- Guidance: Asking for protection from temptation and evil.

Practical Applications:

- Regular Prayer: Making prayer a daily habit, following the model Jesus provided.

- Dependence on God: Trusting God for our daily needs and guidance.

Judging Others

Jesus warned against hypocritical judgment and encouraged self-examination before correcting others.

Matthew 7:1-5:

"Judge not, that ye be not judged. For with what judgment ye judge, ye shall be judged: and with what measure ye mete, it shall be measured to you again. And why beholdest thou the mote that is in thy brother's eye, but considerest not the beam that is in thine own eye? Or how wilt thou say to thy brother, Let me pull out the mote out of thine eye; and, behold, a beam is in thine own eye? Thou hypocrite, first cast out the beam out of thine own eye; and then shalt thou see clearly to cast out the mote out of thy brother's eye."

Key Elements:

- Hypocritical Judgment: Condemning others while ignoring one's own faults.

- Self-Examination: Correcting oneself before addressing others' faults.

Practical Applications:

- Avoiding Judgment: Refraining from harsh judgments and being mindful of our own shortcomings.

- Self-Reflection: Regularly examining our own lives and seeking to grow in holiness.

Jesus' parables, miracles, and the Sermon on the Mount provide rich, multifaceted teachings that reveal the nature of God's kingdom and offer practical guidance for living out our faith. The parables challenge us to reflect on our hearts and actions, the miracles demonstrate Jesus' divine power and compassion, and the Sermon on the Mount calls us to a higher standard of righteousness, love, and humility.

As we embrace these teachings and apply them in our daily lives, we are transformed into the image of Christ, becoming salt and light in the world. By living out the lessons from Jesus' life, we can positively impact our communities and reflect the love and truth of God in all we do. The teachings of Jesus continue to resonate, offering timeless wisdom and hope for believers navigating the complexities of the world.

Core Messages of Love, Forgiveness, and Salvation

At the heart of Jesus Christ's teachings are the core messages of love, forgiveness, and salvation. These themes are central to the Christian faith, providing the foundation for how believers are to relate to God, each other, and the world. In this chapter, we will explore these core messages as presented in the teachings of Jesus, their theological significance, and their practical applications in the lives of believers.

The Message of Love

The Greatest Commandment

Jesus emphasized love as the greatest commandment, summarizing the entire Law and the Prophets with the call to love God and love others.

Matthew 22:37-40:

"Jesus said unto him, Thou shalt love the Lord thy God with all thy heart, and with all thy soul, and with all thy mind. This is the first and great commandment. And the second is like unto it, Thou shalt love thy neighbour as thyself. On these two commandments hang all the law and the prophets."

Key Elements:

- Love for God: A wholehearted devotion to God.

- Love for Neighbor: Treating others with the same care and respect as oneself.

Practical Applications:

- Daily Devotion: Engaging in prayer, worship, and Bible study to deepen one's relationship with God.

- Acts of Kindness: Demonstrating love through acts of kindness, compassion, and generosity to others.

The New Commandment

Jesus introduced a new commandment that emphasizes the importance of loving one another as He loved us.

John 13:34-35:

"A new commandment I give unto you, That ye love one another; as I have loved you, that ye also love one another. By this shall all men know that ye are my disciples, if ye have love one to another."

Key Elements:

- Love as Jesus Loved: Sacrificial, unconditional love.

- Witness to the World: Demonstrating discipleship through love.

Practical Applications:

- Selfless Love: Putting others' needs before our own and showing sacrificial love.

- Community Building: Fostering a supportive and loving community within the church and beyond.

The Parable of the Good Samaritan

The parable of the Good Samaritan teaches about love and mercy, illustrating the call to love and serve our neighbors regardless of their background.

Luke 10:30-37:

"And Jesus answering said, A certain man went down from Jerusalem to Jericho, and fell among thieves, which stripped him of his raiment, and wounded him, and departed, leaving him half dead. And by chance there came down a certain priest that way: and when he saw him, he passed by on the other side. And likewise a Levite, when he was at the place, came and looked on him, and passed by on the other side. But a certain Samaritan, as he journeyed, came where he was: and when he saw him, he had compassion on him, And went to him, and bound up his wounds, pouring in oil and wine, and set him on his own beast, and brought him to an inn, and took care of him. And on the morrow when he departed, he took out two pence, and gave them to the host, and said unto him, Take care of him; and whatsoever thou spendest more, when I come again, I will repay thee. Which now of these three, thinkest thou, was neighbour unto him that fell among the thieves? And he said, He that shewed mercy on him. Then said Jesus unto him, Go, and do thou likewise."

Key Elements:

- Compassion: Acting out of love and care for others.

- Neighbor: Redefining neighbor as anyone in need.

Practical Applications:

- Showing Mercy: Actively seeking to help those in need, regardless of their social status or ethnicity.

- Loving Unconditionally: Embracing the call to love and serve all people.

The Message of Forgiveness

Teaching on Forgiveness

Jesus taught that forgiveness should be limitless, reflecting the boundless forgiveness we receive from God.

Matthew 18:21-22:

"Then came Peter to him, and said, Lord, how oft shall my brother sin against me, and I forgive him? till seven times? Jesus saith unto him, I say not unto thee, Until seven times: but, Until seventy times seven."

Key Elements:

- Limitless Forgiveness: Forgiving others repeatedly without keeping count.

Practical Applications:

- Forgiving Others: Practicing forgiveness in our daily interactions, refusing to hold grudges.

Parable of the Unforgiving Servant

Jesus illustrated the importance of forgiveness through the parable of the unforgiving servant, emphasizing the need to forgive as we have been forgiven.

Matthew 18:23-35:

"Therefore is the kingdom of heaven likened unto a certain king, which would take account of his servants. And when he had begun to reckon, one was brought unto him, which owed him ten thousand talents. But forasmuch as he had not to pay, his lord commanded him to be sold, and his wife, and children, and all that he had, and payment to be made. The servant therefore fell down, and worshipped him, saying, Lord, have patience with me, and I will pay thee all. Then the lord of that servant was moved with compassion, and loosed him, and forgave him the debt. But the same servant went out, and found one of his fellowservants, which owed him an hundred pence: and he laid hands on him, and took him by the throat, saying, Pay me that thou owest. And his fellowservant fell down at his feet, and besought him, saying, Have patience with me, and I will pay thee all. And he would not: but went and cast him into prison, till he should pay the debt. So when his fellowservants saw what was done, they were very sorry, and came and told unto their lord all that was done. Then his lord, after that he had called him, said unto him, O thou wicked servant, I forgave thee all that debt, because thou desiredst me: Shouldest not thou also have had compassion on thy fellowservant, even as I had pity on thee? And his lord was wroth, and delivered him to the tormentors, till he should pay all that was due unto him. So likewise shall my heavenly Father do also unto you, if ye from your hearts forgive not every one his brother their trespasses."

Key Elements:

- Compassion: Showing the same compassion and forgiveness we have received from God.

- Consequences of Unforgiveness: The importance of forgiving others to avoid God's judgment.

Practical Applications:

- Forgiving from the Heart: Truly forgiving others, not just outwardly but from the heart.

- Reflecting God's Forgiveness: Extending the grace we have received to others.

Jesus on the Cross

Jesus' ultimate act of forgiveness was demonstrated on the cross when He asked God to forgive those who crucified Him.

Luke 23:34:

"Then said Jesus, Father, forgive them; for they know not what they do. And they parted his raiment, and cast lots."

Key Elements:

- Forgiveness in Suffering: Jesus forgave even in the midst of His suffering.

- Example of Forgiveness: Setting a precedent for believers to forgive under all circumstances.

Practical Applications:

- Forgiving in Difficult Times: Practicing forgiveness even when it is challenging.

- Following Jesus' Example: Emulating Jesus' attitude of forgiveness in our own lives.

The Message of Salvation

The Necessity of Being Born Again

Jesus emphasized the necessity of being born again to enter the kingdom of God, signifying a spiritual rebirth.

John 3:3:

"Jesus answered and said unto him, Verily, verily, I say unto thee, Except a man be born again, he cannot see the kingdom of God."

Key Elements:

- Spiritual Rebirth: A transformation and renewal through the Holy Spirit.

Practical Applications:

- Seeking Transformation: Allowing the Holy Spirit to transform our hearts and minds.

- Living as New Creations: Embracing our identity as new creations in Christ.

The Good Shepherd

Jesus described Himself as the Good Shepherd who lays down His life for the sheep, emphasizing His sacrificial love and care.

John 10:11:

"I am the good shepherd: the good shepherd giveth his life for the sheep."

Key Elements:

- Sacrificial Love: Jesus' willingness to die for humanity.

- Guidance and Protection: Jesus' role in guiding and protecting His followers.

Practical Applications:

- Trusting in Jesus' Care: Relying on Jesus for guidance and protection.

- Following the Shepherd: Living in obedience to Jesus' teachings.

The Way, the Truth, and the Life

Jesus declared Himself to be the only way to the Father, emphasizing that salvation is found exclusively through Him.

John 14:6:

"Jesus saith unto him, I am the way, the truth, and the life: no man cometh unto the Father, but by me."

Key Elements:

- Exclusive Path to Salvation: Jesus as the only way to God.

- Source of Truth and Life: Jesus as the embodiment of truth and giver of eternal life.

Practical Applications:

- Faith in Jesus: Trusting in Jesus alone for salvation.

- Living by Truth: Following Jesus' teachings as the ultimate truth.

The Great Commission

Jesus commissioned His disciples to spread the message of salvation to all nations, emphasizing the global scope of the gospel.

Matthew 28:19-20:

"Go ye therefore, and teach all nations, baptizing them in the name of the Father, and of the Son, and of the Holy Ghost: Teaching them to observe all things whatsoever I have commanded you: and, lo, I am with you always, even unto the end of the world. Amen."

Key Elements:

- Global Mission: Spreading the gospel to all nations.

- Teaching and Baptizing: Making disciples and baptizing them.

Practical Applications:

- Sharing the Gospel: Actively participating in evangelism and mission work.

- Discipleship: Teaching and mentoring others in the faith.

The core messages of love, forgiveness, and salvation are central to Jesus Christ's teachings and the Christian faith. These messages provide a foundation for how believers are to relate to God, each other, and the world. By embracing these teachings, we can live lives that reflect God's love, grace, and redemptive power.

As we apply these core messages in our daily lives, we are called to love unconditionally, forgive limitlessly, and share the message of salvation with others. The teachings of Jesus continue to resonate, offering timeless wisdom and hope for believers navigating the complexities of the world. Through love, forgiveness, and the assurance of salvation, we can make a profound impact on our communities and bring glory to God in all that we do.

CHAPTER 08

____

THE KINGDOM OF GOD

Central to the teachings of Jesus Christ is the concept of the Kingdom of God. This kingdom is not merely a future reality but a present spiritual realm where God reigns supreme. Throughout His ministry, Jesus taught extensively about the nature, values, and implications of God's kingdom. In this chapter, we will explore Jesus' teachings on the Kingdom of God, examining its characteristics, parables, and the transformative impact it has on the lives of believers.

The Nature of the Kingdom of God

The Kingdom is Near

Jesus began His public ministry with the proclamation that the Kingdom of God is near, urging people to repent and believe the good news.

Mark 1:14-15:

"Now after that John was put in prison, Jesus came into Galilee, preaching the gospel of the kingdom of God, And saying, The time is fulfilled, and the kingdom of God is at hand: repent ye, and believe the gospel."

Key Elements:

- Imminence: The kingdom is close at hand, requiring an immediate response.

- Repentance and Faith: A call to turn from sin and embrace the gospel.

Practical Applications:

- Repentance: Continually examining our lives and turning away from sin.

- Believing the Gospel: Embracing the message of Jesus and living by faith.

The Kingdom is Within You

Jesus emphasized that the Kingdom of God is not a physical realm but a spiritual reality that resides within believers.

Luke 17:20-21:

"And when he was demanded of the Pharisees, when the kingdom of God should come, he answered them and said, The kingdom of God cometh not with observation:

Neither shall they say, Lo here! or, lo there! for, behold, the kingdom of God is within you."

Key Elements:

- Spiritual Realm: The kingdom exists within the hearts of believers.

- Inner Transformation: Emphasis on the inward change brought by the Holy Spirit.

Practical Applications:

- Cultivating Inner Life: Focusing on spiritual growth and developing a deep relationship with God.

- Living Out Kingdom Values: Reflecting the principles of the kingdom in our daily actions and attitudes.

Parables of the Kingdom

The Parable of the Mustard Seed

Jesus used the parable of the mustard seed to illustrate the surprising growth and expansive nature of the Kingdom of God.

Matthew 13:31-32:

"Another parable put he forth unto them, saying, The kingdom of heaven is like to a grain of mustard seed, which a man took, and sowed in his field: Which indeed is the least of all seeds: but when it is grown, it is the greatest among herbs, and becometh a tree, so that the birds of the air come and lodge in the branches thereof."

Key Elements:

- Small Beginnings: The kingdom starts small but grows significantly.

- Expansive Growth: The kingdom's growth impacts the world positively.

Practical Applications:

- Faith in Small Beginnings: Trusting that even small acts of faith and obedience can lead to significant outcomes.

- Participating in Kingdom Growth: Engaging in activities that promote the kingdom's expansion, such as evangelism and service.

The Parable of the Leaven

This parable illustrates how the Kingdom of God influences and transforms the world, much like leaven affects dough.

Matthew 13:33:

"Another parable spake he unto them; The kingdom of heaven is like unto leaven, which a woman took, and hid in three measures of meal, till the whole was leavened."

Key Elements:

- Transformative Influence: The kingdom permeates and transforms society.

- Subtle but Powerful: The kingdom's influence may be hidden but is powerful and pervasive.

Practical Applications:

- Being Agents of Change: Allowing our lives to influence and transform our surroundings positively.

- Patiently Awaiting Growth: Trusting in the transformative power of the kingdom, even when its effects are not immediately visible.

The Parable of the Hidden Treasure and the Pearl

These parables emphasize the incomparable value of the Kingdom of God and the joy of discovering and obtaining it.

Matthew 13:44-46:

"Again, the kingdom of heaven is like unto treasure hid in a field; the which when a man hath found, he hideth, and for joy thereof goeth and selleth all that he hath, and buyeth that field. Again, the kingdom of heaven is like unto a merchant man, seeking goodly pearls: Who, when he had found one pearl of great price, went and sold all that he had, and bought it."

Key Elements:

- Incomparable Value: The kingdom is worth more than anything else we possess.

- Joyful Sacrifice: The discovery of the kingdom brings immense joy, leading to a willingness to give up everything for it.

Practical Applications:

- Valuing the Kingdom: Prioritizing the kingdom above all other pursuits and possessions.

- Joyful Commitment: Embracing the sacrifices required to follow Jesus with joy and gratitude.

Characteristics of the Kingdom

Righteousness, Peace, and Joy

The Kingdom of God is characterized by righteousness, peace, and joy in the Holy Spirit, reflecting the nature of God's rule.

Romans 14:17:

"For the kingdom of God is not meat and drink; but righteousness, and peace, and joy in the Holy Ghost."

Key Elements:

- Righteousness: Living in accordance with God's standards.

- Peace: Experiencing harmony and reconciliation with God and others.

- Joy: Finding deep and abiding joy in the Holy Spirit.

Practical Applications:

- Pursuing Righteousness: Striving to live lives that reflect God's character and commands.

- Promoting Peace: Working towards reconciliation and harmony in our relationships and communities.

- Cultivating Joy: Finding joy in our relationship with God and the work of the Holy Spirit in our lives.

Servanthood and Humility

Jesus taught that greatness in the Kingdom of God is marked by servanthood and humility, contrasting the world's view of power and authority.

Mark 10:42-45:

"But Jesus called them to him, and saith unto them, Ye know that they which are accounted to rule over the Gentiles exercise lordship over them; and their great ones exercise authority upon them. But so shall it not be among you: but whosoever will be great among you, shall be your minister: And whosoever of you will be the chiefest, shall be servant of all. For even the Son of man came not to be ministered unto, but to minister, and to give his life a ransom for many."

Key Elements:

- Servanthood: True greatness is found in serving others.

- Humility: Valuing others above oneself and embracing a humble attitude.

Practical Applications:

- Serving Others: Actively seeking ways to serve and support those around us.

- Embracing Humility: Cultivating a humble heart and attitude in all our interactions.

Faith and Childlikeness

Jesus emphasized the importance of faith and a childlike attitude in receiving and entering the Kingdom of God.

Mark 10:15:

"Verily I say unto you, Whosoever shall not receive the kingdom of God as a little child, he shall not enter therein."

Key Elements:

- Faith: Trusting in God with a simple and sincere faith.

- Childlikeness: Approaching God with humility, dependence, and openness.

Practical Applications:

- Trusting God Fully: Cultivating a simple, unwavering trust in God's goodness and faithfulness.

- Maintaining Openness: Being open to God's leading and teaching, just as a child is receptive to learning.

The Impact of the Kingdom

Transformation of Individuals

The Kingdom of God brings about a profound transformation in the lives of individuals, renewing their hearts and minds.

2 Corinthians 5:17:

"Therefore if any man be in Christ, he is a new creature: old things are passed away; behold, all things are become new."

Key Elements:

- New Creation: Believers are transformed into new creations in Christ.

- Renewal: Continuous renewal of the heart and mind through the Holy Spirit.

Practical Applications:

- Embracing Transformation: Allowing the Holy Spirit to transform our character and actions.

- Living as New Creations: Reflecting our new identity in Christ in every aspect of our lives.

Establishing Justice and Compassion

The Kingdom of God calls believers to establish justice and show compassion, reflecting God's heart for the marginalized and oppressed.

Matthew 25:34-40:

"Then shall the King say unto them on his right hand, Come, ye blessed of my Father, inherit the kingdom prepared for you from the foundation of the world: For I was an hungred, and ye gave me meat: I was thirsty, and ye gave me drink: I was a stranger, and ye took me in: Naked, and ye clothed me: I was sick, and ye visited me: I was in prison, and ye came unto me. Then shall the righteous answer him, saying, Lord, when saw we thee an hungred, and fed thee? or thirsty, and gave thee drink? When saw we thee a stranger, and took thee in? or naked, and clothed thee? Or when saw we thee sick, or in prison, and came unto thee? And the King shall answer and say unto them, Verily I say unto you, Inasmuch as ye have done it unto one of the least of these my brethren, ye have done it unto me."

Key Elements:

- Justice: Acting justly and advocating for the oppressed.

- Compassion: Showing love and care for those in need.

Practical Applications:

- Pursuing Justice: Working towards fairness and justice in our communities and society.

- Practicing Compassion: Actively showing love and care to those who are marginalized and in need.

Proclaiming the Kingdom

Believers are called to proclaim the message of the Kingdom of God, sharing the good news of Jesus Christ with others.

Matthew 28:19-20:

"Go ye therefore, and teach all nations, baptizing them in the name of the Father, and of the Son, and of the Holy Ghost: Teaching them to observe all things whatsoever I have commanded you: and, lo, I am with you always, even unto the end of the world. Amen."

Key Elements:

- Proclamation: Sharing the message of the kingdom with others.

- Discipleship: Teaching and nurturing new believers in their faith.

Practical Applications:

- Evangelism: Actively sharing the gospel with those around us.

- Mentorship: Discipling and mentoring others in their walk with Christ.

Jesus' teachings about the Kingdom of God reveal a profound spiritual reality that transforms individuals and societies. This kingdom is characterized by righteousness, peace, joy, servanthood, humility, faith, and childlikeness. Through parables, Jesus illustrated the nature and value of the kingdom, calling His followers to live out its principles and share its message.

As believers, we are called to embrace the kingdom in our hearts, reflect its values in our lives, and actively work towards its expansion. The Kingdom of God continues to offer hope, purpose, and direction, guiding us as we navigate the complexities of the world and seek to live out our faith in tangible ways.

Parallels with Daniel's Visions of God's Everlasting Kingdom

The teachings of Jesus about the Kingdom of God closely parallel the visions of the everlasting kingdom described in the Book of Daniel. These parallels not only highlight the continuity of God's plan throughout the Scriptures but also affirm the divinity of Jesus and His central role in the fulfillment of these prophecies. In this chapter, we will explore these parallels, drawing on Bible verses, expository study, and exhaustive Strong's Concordance to provide a comprehensive understanding of the Kingdom of God as revealed in both the Old and New Testaments.

Daniel's Vision of the Everlasting Kingdom

The Vision of the Four Beasts and the Son of Man

In Daniel 7, the prophet Daniel receives a vision of four great beasts representing kingdoms of the earth, followed by a vision of the "Son of Man" who is given an everlasting dominion.

Daniel 7:13-14:

"I saw in the night visions, and, behold, one like the Son of man came with the clouds of heaven, and came to the Ancient of days, and they brought him near before him. And there was given him dominion, and glory, and a kingdom, that all people, nations, and languages, should serve him: his dominion is an everlasting dominion, which shall not pass away, and his kingdom that which shall not be destroyed."

Key Elements:

- Son of Man: A messianic figure who receives everlasting dominion.

- Everlasting Dominion: A kingdom that will never be destroyed.

- Universal Reign: A kingdom that encompasses all people, nations, and languages.

Strong's Concordance:

- Son (בַּר, bar, Strong's H1247): Aramaic term for "son."

- Man (אֱנָשׁ, enash, Strong's H606): Aramaic term for "man."

- Dominion (שָׁלְטָן, sholtan, Strong's H7985): Authority or sovereign power.

- Kingdom (מַלְכוּ, malku, Strong's H4437): Realm or reign.

Jesus' Teachings on the Kingdom of God

The Son of Man in the New Testament

Jesus frequently referred to Himself as the "Son of Man," directly linking His mission and identity to Daniel's vision.

Matthew 24:30:

"And then shall appear the sign of the Son of man in heaven: and then shall all the tribes of the earth mourn, and they shall see the Son of man coming in the clouds of heaven with power and great glory."

Key Elements:

- Son of Man: Jesus' preferred self-designation, emphasizing His role as the messianic figure from Daniel's vision.

- Coming in the Clouds: An explicit reference to Daniel 7:13, highlighting His divine authority and eschatological role.

Strong's Concordance:

- Son of Man (υἱὸς τοῦ ἀνθρώπου, huios tou anthrōpou, Strong's G5207 & G444): Greek term used by Jesus to refer to Himself.

The Everlasting Kingdom

Jesus taught that the Kingdom of God is an everlasting kingdom, consistent with Daniel's vision.

Luke 1:32-33:

"He shall be great, and shall be called the Son of the Highest: and the Lord God shall give unto him the throne of his father David: And he shall reign over the house of Jacob for ever; and of his kingdom there shall be no end."

Key Elements:

- Everlasting Reign: Jesus' kingdom will never end.

- Throne of David: Jesus fulfills the promise of an eternal Davidic kingdom.

Strong's Concordance:

- Reign (βασιλεύω, basileuō, Strong's G936): To rule as king.

- Kingdom (βασιλεία, basileia, Strong's G932): Realm or reign.

Parallels Between Daniel's Visions and Jesus' Teachings

The Stone that Becomes a Mountain

In Daniel 2, Nebuchadnezzar's dream, interpreted by Daniel, describes a stone that becomes a great mountain and fills the whole earth, symbolizing God's everlasting kingdom.

Daniel 2:34-35:

"Thou sawest till that a stone was cut out without hands, which smote the image upon his feet that were of iron and clay, and brake them to pieces. Then was the iron, the clay, the brass, the silver, and the gold, broken to pieces together, and became like the chaff of the summer threshingfloors; and the wind carried them away, that no place was found for them: and the stone that smote the image became a great mountain, and filled the whole earth."

Key Elements:

- Stone Cut Without Hands: Divine origin of the kingdom.

- Great Mountain: The kingdom's expansive and enduring nature.

Strong's Concordance:

- Stone (אֶבֶן, eben, Strong's H68): Symbolizing Christ and His kingdom.

- Mountain (הַר, har, Strong's H2022): Represents a large, stable, and influential kingdom.

New Testament Fulfillment:

- Matthew 21:42-44: "Jesus saith unto them, Did ye never read in the scriptures, The stone which the builders rejected, the same is become the head of the corner: this is the Lord's doing, and it is marvellous in our eyes? Therefore say I unto you, The kingdom of God shall be taken from you, and given to a nation bringing forth the fruits thereof. And whosoever shall fall on this stone shall be broken: but on whomsoever it shall fall, it will grind him to powder."

Key Elements:

- Jesus as the Stone: Jesus identifies Himself as the cornerstone.

- Kingdom of God: The divine, everlasting kingdom prophesied in Daniel.

The Kingdom Given to the Saints

Daniel's vision also includes the saints receiving the kingdom, a theme echoed in Jesus' teachings.

Daniel 7:18:

"But the saints of the most High shall take the kingdom, and possess the kingdom for ever, even for ever and ever."

Key Elements:

- Saints of the Most High: Believers who inherit the kingdom.

- Everlasting Possession: The eternal nature of the kingdom.

Strong's Concordance:

- Saints (קַדִּישׁ, qaddish, Strong's H6922): Holy ones or believers.

- Possess (חֲסַן, chasan, Strong's H2631): To hold or inherit.

New Testament Fulfillment:

- Matthew 5:5: "Blessed are the meek: for they shall inherit the earth."

- Revelation 5:10: "And hast made us unto our God kings and priests: and we shall reign on the earth."

Key Elements:

- Inheritance: Believers will inherit the kingdom.

- Reigning with Christ: Sharing in Christ's eternal reign.

The Divinity of Jesus in the Kingdom Context

The Son of Man's Divine Authority

Jesus' use of the title "Son of Man" and His descriptions of His authority directly connect Him to the divine figure in Daniel's vision.

Matthew 26:64:

"Jesus saith unto him, Thou hast said: nevertheless I say unto you, Hereafter shall ye see the Son of man sitting on the right hand of power, and coming in the clouds of heaven."

Key Elements:

- Sitting at the Right Hand of Power: A position of divine authority.

- Coming in the Clouds: A direct reference to Daniel's vision, affirming His divinity.

Strong's Concordance:

- Power (δυναμις, dynamis, Strong's G1411): Strength or authority.

- Clouds (νεφέλη, nephelē, Strong's G3507): Symbolizing divine presence.

Jesus' Role as Judge

Jesus also spoke of His role as the ultimate judge, a function associated with divine authority and consistent with the Son of Man's dominion in Daniel's vision.

John 5:22-27:

"For the Father judgeth no man, but hath committed all judgment unto the Son: That all men should honour the Son, even as they honour the Father. He that honoureth not the Son honoureth not the Father which hath sent him. Verily, verily, I say unto you, He that heareth my word, and believeth on him that sent me, hath everlasting life, and shall not come into condemnation; but is passed from death unto life. Verily, verily, I say unto you, The hour is coming, and now is, when the dead shall hear the voice of the Son of God: and they that hear shall live. For as the Father hath life in himself; so hath he given to the Son to have life in himself; And hath given him authority to execute judgment also, because he is the Son of man."

Key Elements:

- All Judgment Committed to the Son: Jesus as the ultimate judge.

- Honor to the Son: Equal honor to the Father and the Son, underscoring Jesus' divinity.

Strong's Concordance:

- Judgment (κρίσις, krisis, Strong's G2920): The process of judging.

- Authority (ἐξουσία, exousia, Strong's G1849): Power or right to act.

The parallels between Jesus' teachings about the Kingdom of God and Daniel's visions of God's everlasting kingdom demonstrate a consistent and unified biblical narrative. Jesus' self-identification as the "Son of Man" and His descriptions of the kingdom underscore His fulfillment of Old Testament prophecies and affirm His divinity. These teachings reveal the nature of the kingdom as a present spiritual reality with a future fulfillment, characterized by righteousness, peace, joy, and eternal dominion.

As believers, understanding these parallels deepens our appreciation for the continuity of God's redemptive plan and the centrality of Jesus in bringing it to fruition. Embracing the kingdom values and living in the light of its eternal truths transforms our lives and aligns us with God's purposes. The Kingdom of God, as revealed through Daniel and fulfilled in Jesus, offers hope, purpose, and direction for all who seek to follow Christ.

Living as Citizens of the Kingdom

Living as citizens of the Kingdom of God involves embodying the values and principles that Jesus taught. This entails a transformation of character, priorities, and actions that reflect the reign of God in our lives. In this chapter, we will explore what it means to live as citizens of the Kingdom, drawing on Bible verses, expository study, and insights from Strong's Concordance to provide a comprehensive understanding of this vital aspect of Christian living.

The Characteristics of Kingdom Citizens

The Beatitudes: Kingdom Values

The Beatitudes, found in the Sermon on the Mount, describe the attitudes and behaviors that characterize the citizens of God's Kingdom.

Matthew 5:3-12:

"Blessed are the poor in spirit: for theirs is the kingdom of heaven. Blessed are they that mourn: for they shall be comforted. Blessed are the meek: for they shall inherit the earth. Blessed are they which do hunger and thirst after righteousness: for they shall be filled. Blessed are the merciful: for they shall obtain mercy. Blessed are the pure in heart: for they shall see God. Blessed are the peacemakers: for they shall be called the children of God. Blessed are they which are persecuted for righteousness' sake: for theirs is the kingdom of heaven. Blessed are ye when men shall revile you, and persecute you, and shall say all manner of evil against you falsely, for my sake. Rejoice, and be exceeding glad: for great is your reward in heaven: for so persecuted they the prophets which were before you."

Key Elements:

- Poor in Spirit (πτωχός, ptochos, Strong's G4434): Humility and dependence on God.

- Mourning (πενθέω, pentheō, Strong's G3996): Sorrow for sin and suffering.

- Meekness (πραΰς, praus, Strong's G4239): Gentleness and self-control.

- Hunger and Thirst for Righteousness (δικαιοσύνη, dikaiosynē, Strong's G1343): Deep desire for justice and holiness.

- Merciful (ἐλεήμων, eleēmōn, Strong's G1655): Compassionate and forgiving.

- Pure in Heart (καθαρός, katharos, Strong's G2513): Sincerity and moral integrity.

- Peacemakers (εἰρηνοποιός, eirēnopoios, Strong's G1518): Promoting peace and reconciliation.

- Persecuted for Righteousness' Sake (διώκω, diōkō, Strong's G1377): Enduring suffering for doing what is right.

Practical Applications:

- Cultivating Humility: Recognizing our need for God and relying on His strength.

- Seeking Justice and Holiness: Striving for righteousness in our personal and communal lives.

- Showing Compassion: Extending mercy and forgiveness to others.

- Promoting Peace: Working towards reconciliation and harmony in our relationships and communities.

The Fruit of the Spirit

Paul's letter to the Galatians outlines the characteristics that the Holy Spirit produces in the lives of believers, reflecting the values of the Kingdom.

Galatians 5:22-23:

"But the fruit of the Spirit is love, joy, peace, longsuffering, gentleness, goodness, faith, Meekness, temperance: against such there is no law."

Key Elements:

- Love (ἀγάπη, agapē, Strong's G26): Selfless, sacrificial affection.

- Joy (χαρά, chara, Strong's G5479): Deep and abiding happiness.

- Peace (εἰρήνη, eirēnē, Strong's G1515): Harmony and tranquility.

- Longsuffering (μακροθυμία, makrothymia, Strong's G3115): Patience and endurance.

- Gentleness (χρηστότης, chrēstotēs, Strong's G5544): Kindness and compassion.

- Goodness (ἀγαθωσύνη, agathōsynē, Strong's G19): Moral excellence and virtue.

- Faith (πίστις, pistis, Strong's G4102): Trust and faithfulness.

- Meekness (πραΰτης, praotēs, Strong's G4240): Humility and gentleness.

- Temperance (ἐγκράτεια, enkrateia, Strong's G1466): Self-control and discipline.

Practical Applications:

- Developing Love and Joy: Fostering deep affection for others and finding joy in God's presence.

- Practicing Patience and Kindness: Being patient with others and showing kindness in our interactions.

- Exercising Self-Control: Maintaining discipline in our thoughts, words, and actions.

Living Out Kingdom Priorities

Seeking First the Kingdom

Jesus taught that the Kingdom of God should be the primary pursuit in the lives of His followers, promising that God will provide for their needs.

Matthew 6:33:

"But seek ye first the kingdom of God, and his righteousness; and all these things shall be added unto you."

Key Elements:

- Primary Pursuit (ζητέω, zēteō, Strong's G2212): Making the kingdom the foremost priority.

- God's Provision (προστίθημι, prostithēmi, Strong's G4369): Trusting that God will meet our needs as we prioritize His kingdom.

Practical Applications:

- Prioritizing Spiritual Growth: Investing time in prayer, Bible study, and worship.

- Trusting God's Provision: Relying on God to provide for our physical and material needs.

Storing Up Treasures in Heaven

Jesus emphasized the importance of focusing on eternal treasures rather than temporal wealth.

Matthew 6:19-21:

"Lay not up for yourselves treasures upon earth, where moth and rust doth corrupt, and where thieves break through and steal: But lay up for yourselves treasures in heaven, where neither moth nor rust doth corrupt, and where thieves do not break through nor steal: For where your treasure is, there will your heart be also."

Key Elements:

- Eternal Treasures (θησαυρός, thēsauros, Strong's G2344): Valuing what has eternal significance.

- Heart's Focus (καρδία, kardia, Strong's G2588): Our priorities reflect our true values.

Practical Applications:

- Investing in Eternity: Engaging in activities that have eternal significance, such as sharing the gospel and serving others.

- Evaluating Priorities: Regularly assessing where our time, energy, and resources are directed.

The Conduct of Kingdom Citizens

Living Righteously

Paul exhorted believers to live lives that are worthy of the Kingdom of God, characterized by righteousness and holiness.

Ephesians 4:1-3:

"I therefore, the prisoner of the Lord, beseech you that ye walk worthy of the vocation wherewith ye are called, With all lowliness and meekness, with longsuffering, forbearing one another in love; Endeavouring to keep the unity of the Spirit in the bond of peace."

Key Elements:

- Worthy Walk (ἀξίως, axiōs, Strong's G516): Living in a manner that reflects our calling.

- Unity and Peace (ἑνότης, henotēs, Strong's G1775 and εἰρήνη, eirēnē, Strong's G1515): Maintaining unity and peace within the body of Christ.

Practical Applications:

- Practicing Humility and Patience: Treating others with gentleness and patience.

- Promoting Unity: Working towards unity and harmony within the church.

Bearing Witness to the Kingdom

Jesus commissioned His followers to be His witnesses, proclaiming the good news of the Kingdom to all nations.

Acts 1:8:

"But ye shall receive power, after that the Holy Ghost is come upon you: and ye shall be witnesses unto me both in Jerusalem, and in all Judaea, and in Samaria, and unto the uttermost part of the earth."

Key Elements:

- Witnesses (μάρτυς, martys, Strong's G3144): Testifying to the truth of the gospel.

- Empowerment by the Holy Spirit (δύναμις, dynamis, Strong's G1411): Relying on the Holy Spirit for power and guidance.

Practical Applications:

- Sharing the Gospel: Actively seeking opportunities to share the message of Jesus with others.

- Relying on the Holy Spirit: Depending on the Holy Spirit for boldness and wisdom in witnessing.

Serving Others

Jesus taught that greatness in the Kingdom of God is found in serving others, following His example of humble service.

Mark 10:42-45:

"But Jesus called them to him, and saith unto them, Ye know that they which are accounted to rule over the Gentiles exercise lordship over them; and their great ones exercise authority upon them. But so shall it not be among you: but whosoever will be great among you, shall be your minister: And whosoever of you will be the chiefest, shall be servant of all. For even the Son of man came not to be ministered unto, but to minister, and to give his life a ransom for many."

Key Elements:

- Servanthood (διάκονος, diakonos, Strong's G1249): Serving others selflessly.

- Example of Jesus: Emulating Jesus' attitude of humility and service.

Practical Applications:

- Serving in Humility: Seeking to serve others without seeking recognition or reward.

- Following Jesus' Example: Embracing opportunities to serve others in practical ways.

The Hope of Kingdom Citizens

The Coming Kingdom

Believers live in the hope of the coming Kingdom of God, where Jesus will reign fully and finally.

Revelation 21:1-4:

"And I saw a new heaven and a new earth: for the first heaven and the first earth were passed away; and there was no more sea. And I John saw the holy city, new Jerusalem, coming down from God out of heaven, prepared as a bride adorned for her husband. And I heard a great voice out of heaven saying, Behold, the tabernacle of God is with men, and he will dwell with them, and they shall be his people, and God himself shall be with them, and be their God. And God shall wipe away all tears from their eyes; and there shall be no more death, neither sorrow, nor crying, neither shall there be any more pain: for the former things are passed away."

Key Elements:

- New Heaven and New Earth (καινός, kainos, Strong's G2537 and γῆ, gē, Strong's G1093): The renewed creation.

- God's Dwelling with Humanity: The ultimate fulfillment of God's presence with His people.

Practical Applications:

- Living with Hope: Maintaining a future-oriented perspective that inspires perseverance and faithfulness.

- Preparing for the Kingdom: Living in a way that reflects our anticipation of the coming Kingdom.

Living as citizens of the Kingdom of God involves embodying the values and principles taught by Jesus. It requires a transformation of character, priorities, and actions that reflect God's reign in our lives. By cultivating the attitudes described in the Beatitudes, displaying the fruit of the Spirit, prioritizing the Kingdom, and bearing witness to its truth, we demonstrate our allegiance to God's Kingdom.

As we live out these values, we not only experience personal transformation but also become agents of change in our communities and the world. The hope of the coming Kingdom inspires us to live faithfully, anticipating the day when Jesus will fully establish His reign. Embracing our identity as Kingdom citizens, we strive to reflect God's love, justice, and righteousness in all we do, bringing glory to God and drawing others to His Kingdom.

CHAPTER 09

THE SECOND COMING

The Second Coming of Jesus Christ is a pivotal event in Christian eschatology, marking the culmination of God's redemptive plan and the fulfillment of biblical prophecies. Both the Book of Daniel and the teachings of Jesus provide profound insights into the end times. In this chapter, we will explore the prophecies of Daniel and Jesus regarding the end times, examining their implications and the hope they offer to believers. We will use Bible verses, expository study, and insights from Strong's Concordance to provide a comprehensive understanding of these prophecies.

Prophecies in the Book of Daniel

The Vision of the Seventy Weeks

Daniel's prophecy of the seventy weeks outlines a timeline leading to the coming of the Messiah and the end times.

Daniel 9:24-27:

"Seventy weeks are determined upon thy people and upon thy holy city, to finish the transgression, and to make an end of sins, and to make reconciliation for iniquity, and to bring in everlasting righteousness, and to seal up the vision and prophecy, and to anoint the most Holy. Know therefore and understand, that from the going forth of the commandment to restore and to build Jerusalem unto the Messiah the Prince shall be seven weeks, and threescore and two weeks: the street shall be built again, and the wall, even in troublous times. And after threescore and two weeks shall Messiah be cut off, but not for himself: and the people of the prince that shall come shall destroy the city and the sanctuary; and the end thereof shall be with a flood, and unto the end of the war desolations are determined. And he shall confirm the covenant with many for one week: and in the midst of the week he shall cause the sacrifice and the oblation to cease, and for the overspreading of abominations he shall make it desolate, even until the consummation, and that determined shall be poured upon the desolate."

Key Elements:

- Seventy Weeks (שָׁבוּעַ, shabuwa, Strong's H7620): Represents 490 years.

- Messiah Cut Off: The crucifixion of Jesus.

- Destruction of Jerusalem: Foretells the Roman destruction of the city in 70 AD.

- Final Week: The end times period involving the Antichrist and ultimate redemption.

Practical Applications:

- Understanding God's Timeline: Recognizing the fulfillment of prophecies and God's sovereign plan.

- Anticipating the Future: Living with expectancy and preparedness for the end times.

The Vision of the Four Beasts

Daniel's vision of the four beasts represents successive empires and culminates in the establishment of God's eternal kingdom.

Daniel 7:2-14:

"Daniel spake and said, I saw in my vision by night, and, behold, the four winds of the heaven strove upon the great sea. And four great beasts came up from the sea, diverse one from another. The first was like a lion, and had eagle's wings: I beheld till the wings thereof were plucked, and it was lifted up from the earth, and made stand upon the feet as a man, and a man's heart was given to it. And behold another beast, a second, like to a bear, and it raised up itself on one side, and it had three ribs in the mouth of it between the teeth of it: and they said thus unto it, Arise, devour much flesh. After this I beheld, and lo another, like a leopard, which had upon the back of it four wings of a fowl; the beast had also four heads; and dominion was given to it. After this I saw in the night visions, and behold a fourth beast, dreadful and terrible, and strong exceedingly; and it had great iron teeth: it devoured and brake in pieces, and stamped the residue with the feet of it: and it was diverse from all the beasts that were before it; and it had ten horns. I considered the horns, and, behold, there came up among them another little horn, before whom there were three of the first horns plucked up by the roots: and, behold, in this horn were eyes like the eyes of man, and a mouth speaking great things. I beheld till the thrones were cast down, and the Ancient of days did sit, whose garment was white as snow, and the hair of his head like the pure wool: his throne was like the fiery flame, and his wheels as burning fire. A fiery stream issued and came forth from before him: thousand thousands ministered unto him, and ten thousand times ten thousand stood before him: the judgment was set, and the books were opened. I beheld then because of the voice of the great words which the horn spake: I beheld even till the beast was slain, and his body destroyed, and given to the burning flame. As concerning the rest of the beasts, they had their dominion taken away: yet their lives were prolonged for a season and time. I saw in the night visions, and, behold, one like the Son of man came with the clouds of heaven, and came to the Ancient of days, and they brought him near before him. And there was given him dominion, and glory, and a kingdom, that all people, nations, and languages, should serve him: his dominion is an everlasting dominion, which shall not pass away, and his kingdom that which shall not be destroyed."

Key Elements:

- Four Beasts: Represent successive empires.

- Son of Man: Receives eternal dominion from the Ancient of Days.

Strong's Concordance:

- Beasts (חֵיוָא, cheva, Strong's H2423): Symbolic of kingdoms or empires.

- Son of Man (אֱנָשׁ בַּר, bar enash, Strong's H1247 & H606): A messianic title referring to Jesus.

- Ancient of Days (יוֹמִין עַתִּיק, attiyq yomiyn, Strong's H6268 & H3118): A title for God emphasizing His eternal nature.

Practical Applications:

- Recognizing Divine Authority: Acknowledging God's sovereignty over earthly kingdoms.

- Living with Hope: Anticipating the ultimate establishment of God's eternal kingdom.

Jesus' Teachings on the End Times

The Olivet Discourse

In the Olivet Discourse, Jesus provides a detailed description of the signs of the end times and His return.

Matthew 24:3-31:

"And as he sat upon the mount of Olives, the disciples came unto him privately, saying, Tell us, when shall these things be? and what shall be the sign of thy coming, and of the end of the world? And Jesus answered and said unto them, Take heed that no man deceive you. For many shall come in my name, saying, I am Christ; and shall deceive many. And ye shall hear of wars and rumours of wars: see that ye be not troubled: for all these things must come to pass, but the end is not yet. For nation shall rise against nation, and kingdom against kingdom: and there shall be famines, and pestilences, and earthquakes, in divers places. All these are the beginning of sorrows. Then shall they deliver you up to be afflicted, and shall kill you: and ye shall be hated of all nations for my name's sake. And then shall many be offended, and shall betray one another, and shall hate one another. And many false prophets shall rise, and shall deceive many. And because iniquity shall abound, the love of many shall wax cold. But he that shall endure unto the end, the same shall be saved. And this gospel of the kingdom shall be preached in all the world for a witness unto all nations; and then shall the end come. When ye therefore shall see the abomination of desolation, spoken of by Daniel the prophet, stand in the holy place, (whoso readeth, let him understand:) Then let them which be in Judaea flee into the mountains: Let him which is on the housetop not come down to take any thing out of his house: Neither let him which is in the field return back to take his clothes. And woe unto them that are with child, and to them that give suck in those days! But pray ye that your flight be not in the winter, neither on the sabbath day: For then shall be great tribulation, such as was not since the beginning of the world to this time, no, nor ever shall be. And except those days should be shortened, there should no flesh be saved: but for the elect's sake those days shall be shortened. Then if any man shall say unto you, Lo, here is Christ, or there; believe it not. For there shall arise false Christs, and false prophets, and shall shew great signs and wonders; insomuch that, if it were possible, they shall deceive the very elect. Behold, I have told you before. Wherefore if they shall say unto you, Behold, he is in the desert; go not forth: behold, he is in the secret chambers; believe it not. For as the lightning cometh out of the east, and shineth even unto the west; so shall also the coming of the Son of man be. For wheresoever the carcase is, there will the eagles be gathered together. Immediately after the tribulation of those days shall the sun be darkened, and the moon shall not give her light, and the stars shall fall from heaven, and the powers of the heavens shall be shaken: And then shall appear the sign of the Son of man in heaven: and then shall all the tribes of the earth mourn, and they shall see the Son of man coming in the clouds of heaven with power and great glory. And he shall send his angels with a great sound of a trumpet, and they shall gather together his elect from the four winds, from one end of heaven to the other."

Key Elements:

- Signs of the End: Deception, wars, famines, earthquakes, and persecution.

- Abomination of Desolation (βδέλυγμα τῆς ἐρημώσεως, bdelugma tēs erēmōseōs, Strong's G946 & G2050): Refers to a sacrilegious event prophesied by Daniel.

- Great Tribulation (θλῖψις, thlipsis, Strong's G2347): A period of unprecedented suffering.

- Coming of the Son of Man: Jesus' return in glory.

Practical Applications:

- Staying Vigilant: Being aware of the signs and remaining faithful.

- Enduring Persecution: Trusting in God's promises during times of trial.

The Parable of the Fig Tree

Jesus used the parable of the fig tree to illustrate the importance of recognizing the signs of the end times and being prepared.

Matthew 24:32-35:

"Now learn a parable of the fig tree; When his branch is yet tender, and putteth forth leaves, ye know that summer is nigh: So likewise ye, when ye shall see all these things, know that it is near, even at the doors. Verily I say unto you, This generation shall not pass, till all these things be fulfilled. Heaven and earth shall pass away, but my words shall not pass away."

Key Elements:

- Fig Tree (συκῆ, sykē, Strong's G4808): Symbolizes the ability to discern the times.

- Signs of the Times: Recognizing the indicators of Jesus' return.

Practical Applications:

- Discerning the Times: Being attentive to the signs of Jesus' return.

- Living Prepared: Living each day in readiness for the Second Coming.

The Parable of the Ten Virgins

This parable emphasizes the need for vigilance and preparedness for the coming of the bridegroom, representing Jesus.

Matthew 25:1-13:

"Then shall the kingdom of heaven be likened unto ten virgins, which took their lamps, and went forth to meet the bridegroom. And five of them were wise, and five were foolish. They that were foolish took their lamps, and took no oil with them: But the wise took oil in their vessels with their lamps. While the bridegroom tarried, they all slumbered and slept. And at midnight there was a cry made, Behold, the bridegroom cometh; go ye out to meet him. Then all those virgins arose, and trimmed their lamps. And the foolish said unto the wise, Give us of your oil; for our lamps are gone out. But the wise answered, saying, Not so; lest there be not enough for us and you: but go ye rather to them that sell, and buy for yourselves. And while they went to buy, the bridegroom came; and they that were ready went in with him to the marriage: and the door was shut. Afterward came also the other virgins, saying, Lord, Lord, open to us. But he answered and said, Verily I say unto you, I know you not.

Watch therefore, for ye know neither the day nor the hour wherein the Son of man cometh."

Key Elements:

- Ten Virgins: Represent believers.

- Lamps and Oil (λύχνος, lychnos, Strong's G3088 & ἔλαιον, elaion, Strong's G1637): Symbolize readiness and spiritual preparedness.

- Bridegroom (νυμφίος, nymphios, Strong's G3566): Represents Jesus.

- Watchfulness (γρηγορέω, grēgoreō, Strong's G1127): The call to be vigilant and prepared.

Practical Applications:

- Maintaining Spiritual Readiness: Cultivating a relationship with God and living in obedience.

- Staying Vigilant: Being alert and prepared for Jesus' return at any time.

The Second Coming and Final Judgment

The Second Coming of Christ

The return of Jesus Christ will be a visible, triumphant event, accompanied by the final judgment.

Revelation 19:11-16:

"And I saw heaven opened, and behold a white horse; and he that sat upon him was called Faithful and True, and in righteousness he doth judge and make war. His eyes were as a flame of fire, and on his head were many crowns; and he had a name written, that no man knew, but he himself. And he was clothed with a vesture dipped in blood: and his name is called The Word of God. And the armies which were in heaven followed him upon white horses, clothed in fine linen, white and clean. And out of his mouth goeth a sharp sword, that with it he should smite the nations: and he shall rule them with a rod of iron: and he treadeth the winepress of the fierceness and wrath of Almighty God. And he hath on his vesture and on his thigh a name written, KING OF KINGS, AND LORD OF LORDS."

Key Elements:

- Faithful and True (πιστός, pistos, Strong's G4103 & ἀληθινός, alēthinos, Strong's G228): Jesus' righteous character.

- The Word of God (λόγος, logos, Strong's G3056): Jesus as the incarnate Word.

- Final Judgment (κρίνω, krinō, Strong's G2919): Jesus' role in executing divine justice.

Practical Applications:

- Living in Hope: Anticipating the return of Christ with confidence and joy.

- Pursuing Righteousness: Striving to live in accordance with God's will in light of the coming judgment.

The Final Judgment

The final judgment will be a time when all people are held accountable for their actions and receive their eternal destinies.

Matthew 25:31-46:

"When the Son of man shall come in his glory, and all the holy angels with him, then shall he sit upon the throne of his glory: And before him shall be gathered all nations: and he shall separate them one from another, as a shepherd divideth his sheep from the goats: And he shall set the sheep on his right hand, but the goats on the left. Then shall the King say unto them on his right hand, Come, ye blessed of my Father, inherit the kingdom prepared for you from the foundation of the world: For I was an hungred, and ye gave me meat: I was thirsty, and ye gave me drink: I was a stranger, and ye took me in: Naked, and ye clothed me: I was sick, and ye visited me: I was in prison, and ye came unto me. Then shall the righteous answer him, saying, Lord, when saw we thee an hungred, and fed thee? or thirsty, and gave thee drink? When saw we thee a stranger, and took thee in? or naked, and clothed thee? Or when saw we thee sick, or in prison, and came unto thee? And the King shall answer and say unto them, Verily I say unto you, Inasmuch as ye have done it unto one of the least of these my brethren, ye have done it unto me. Then shall he say also unto them on the left hand, Depart from me, ye cursed, into everlasting fire, prepared for the devil and his angels: For I was an hungred, and ye gave me no meat: I was thirsty, and ye gave me no drink: I was a stranger, and ye took me not in: naked, and ye clothed me not: sick, and in prison, and ye visited me not. Then shall they also answer him, saying, Lord, when saw we thee an hungred, or athirst, or a stranger, or naked, or sick, or in prison, and did not minister unto thee? Then shall he answer them, saying, Verily I say unto you, Inasmuch as ye did it not to one of the least of these, ye did it not to me. And these shall go away into everlasting punishment: but the righteous into life eternal."

Key Elements:

- Sheep and Goats (πρόβατον, probaton, Strong's G4263 & ἐρίφιον, eriphion, Strong's G2055): Represent the righteous and the wicked.

- Inheriting the Kingdom: Reward for the righteous.

- Everlasting Punishment (κόλασις, kolasis, Strong's G2851): Consequence for the wicked.

Practical Applications:

- Serving Others: Demonstrating our faith through acts of kindness and service.

- Living Righteously: Striving to live in accordance with God's commands, knowing that our actions have eternal significance.

The prophecies of Daniel and Jesus regarding the end times provide profound insights into God's redemptive plan and the culmination of history. These prophecies emphasize the importance of vigilance, preparedness, and faithfulness as we anticipate the Second Coming of Jesus Christ. The teachings of both Daniel and Jesus underscore the certainty of divine judgment and the hope of eternal life for the righteous.

As believers, understanding these prophecies deepens our faith and inspires us to live in a manner worthy of the Kingdom of God. By staying vigilant, enduring trials, and living out our faith through acts of love and service, we prepare ourselves for the glorious return of our Lord. The promise of the Second Coming offers hope and encouragement, reminding us that God's ultimate victory is assured and that His kingdom will be established forever.

The Return of Christ as the Culmination of God's Plan

The return of Christ is the pinnacle of Christian hope and the fulfillment of God's redemptive plan. This event, often referred to as the Second Coming, is prophesied throughout Scripture and signifies the final victory over sin and death, the establishment of God's eternal kingdom, and the ultimate fulfillment of divine promises. In this chapter, we will explore the biblical foundations of the Second Coming, its significance in God's plan, and its implications for believers. We will utilize Bible verses, expository study, and insights from Strong's Concordance to provide a comprehensive understanding of this crucial event.

Biblical Foundations of the Second Coming

Old Testament Prophecies

The Old Testament contains numerous prophecies that point to the Messiah's coming, many of which find their ultimate fulfillment in the Second Coming of Christ.

Isaiah 11:1-10:

"And there shall come forth a rod out of the stem of Jesse, and a Branch shall grow out of his roots: And the spirit of the Lord shall rest upon him, the spirit of wisdom and understanding, the spirit of counsel and might, the spirit of knowledge and of the fear of the Lord; And shall make him of quick understanding in the fear of the Lord: and he shall not judge after the sight of his eyes, neither reprove after the hearing of his ears: But with righteousness shall he judge the poor, and reprove with equity for the meek of the earth: and he shall smite the earth with the rod of his mouth, and with the breath of his lips shall he slay the wicked. And righteousness shall be the girdle of his loins, and faithfulness the girdle of his reins. The wolf also shall dwell with the lamb, and the leopard shall lie down with the kid; and the calf and the young lion and the fatling together; and a little child shall lead them. And the cow and the bear shall feed; their young ones shall lie down together: and the lion shall eat straw like the ox. And the sucking child shall play on the hole of the asp, and the weaned child shall put his hand on the cockatrice' den. They shall not hurt nor destroy in all my holy mountain: for the earth shall be full of the knowledge of the Lord, as the waters cover the sea. And in that day there shall be a root of Jesse, which shall stand for an ensign of the people; to it shall the Gentiles seek: and his rest shall be glorious."

Key Elements:

- Branch from Jesse: A messianic title referring to Jesus.

- Righteous Judgment: The Messiah's role in establishing justice.

- Universal Peace: The transformation of creation under the Messiah's reign.

Strong's Concordance:

- Branch (נֵצֶר, netser, Strong's H5342): A shoot or sprout, symbolizing new life.

- Judge (שָׁפַט, shaphat, Strong's H8199): To govern or rule.

- Peace (שָׁלוֹם, shalom, Strong's H7965): Completeness, welfare, peace.

New Testament Promises

The New Testament elaborates on the Second Coming, providing a clear and detailed account of its significance and the events surrounding it.

Matthew 24:30-31:

"And then shall appear the sign of the Son of man in heaven: and then shall all the tribes of the earth mourn, and they shall see the Son of man coming in the clouds of heaven with power and great glory. And he shall send his angels with a great sound of a trumpet, and they shall gather together his elect from the four winds, from one end of heaven to the other."

Key Elements:

- Son of Man (υἱὸς τοῦ ἀνθρώπου, huios tou anthrōpou, Strong's G5207 & G444): A messianic title used by Jesus.

- Power and Great Glory (δύναμις, dynamis, Strong's G1411 & δόξα, doxa, Strong's G1391): The majesty and authority of Christ's return.

- Gathering of the Elect (ἐκλεκτός, eklektos, Strong's G1588): The final gathering of believers.

The Promise of His Return

Jesus explicitly promised His return, assuring His disciples that He would come again to fulfill God's plan.

John 14:1-3:

"Let not your heart be troubled: ye believe in God, believe also in me. In my Father's house are many mansions: if it were not so, I would have told you. I go to prepare a place for you. And if I go and prepare a place for you, I will come again, and receive you unto myself; that where I am, there ye may be also."

Key Elements:

- Preparation of a Place (ἑτοιμάζω, hetoimazō, Strong's G2090): Jesus preparing a place for His followers.

- Promise of Return (ἔρχομαι, erchomai, Strong's G2064): Jesus' assurance of His Second Coming.

- Eternal Dwelling: Believers being with Jesus forever.

The Significance of the Second Coming

Fulfillment of Prophecy

The Second Coming of Christ fulfills numerous prophecies, demonstrating the reliability of Scripture and God's sovereign plan.

Revelation 19:11-16:

"And I saw heaven opened, and behold a white horse; and he that sat upon him was called Faithful and True, and in righteousness he doth judge and make war. His eyes were as a flame of fire, and on his head were many crowns; and he had a name written, that no man knew, but he himself. And he was clothed with a vesture dipped in blood: and his name is called The Word of God. And the armies which were in heaven followed him upon white horses, clothed in fine linen, white and clean. And out of his mouth goeth a sharp sword, that with it he should smite the nations: and he shall rule them with a rod of iron: and he treadeth the winepress of the fierceness and wrath of Almighty God. And he hath on his vesture and on his thigh a name written, KING OF KINGS, AND LORD OF LORDS."

Key Elements:

- Faithful and True (πιστός, pistos, Strong's G4103 & ἀληθινός, alēthinos, Strong's G228): Titles emphasizing Jesus' trustworthiness and truth.

- Word of God (λόγος τοῦ θεοῦ, logos tou theou, Strong's G3056 & G2316): Jesus as the divine Word.

- King of Kings and Lord of Lords: Jesus' supreme authority.

Practical Applications:

- Trust in Scripture: Confidence in the reliability and fulfillment of biblical prophecies.

- Hope in God's Plan: Assurance of God's sovereign control over history.

The Final Victory Over Evil

The return of Christ marks the final defeat of Satan, sin, and death, ushering in an era of eternal righteousness and peace.

Revelation 20:10:

"And the devil that deceived them was cast into the lake of fire and brimstone, where the beast and the false prophet are, and shall be tormented day and night for ever and ever."

Key Elements:

- Defeat of Satan (διάβολος, diabolos, Strong's G1228): The final judgment of the devil.

- Eternal Punishment (λίμνη τοῦ πυρός, limnē tou pyros, Strong's G3041 & G4442): The lake of fire as the ultimate destination for evil.

Practical Applications:

- Confidence in Victory: Assurance of Christ's ultimate triumph over evil.

- Living in Righteousness: Commitment to living a holy life in anticipation of Christ's return.

The Establishment of God's Eternal Kingdom

Christ's return heralds the full establishment of God's kingdom, where righteousness, peace, and justice will prevail forever.

Revelation 21:1-4:

"And I saw a new heaven and a new earth: for the first heaven and the first earth were passed away; and there was no more sea. And I John saw the holy city, new Jerusalem, coming down from God out of heaven, prepared as a bride adorned for her husband. And I heard a great voice out of heaven saying, Behold, the tabernacle of God is with men, and he will dwell with them, and they shall be his people, and God himself shall be with them, and be their God. And God shall wipe away all tears from their eyes; and there shall be no more death, neither sorrow, nor crying, neither shall there be any more pain: for the former things are passed away."

Key Elements:

- New Heaven and New Earth (καινὸς οὐρανός, kainos ouranos, Strong's G2537 & G3772 and καινὴ γῆ, kainē gē, Strong's G2537 & G1093): The renewed creation.

- New Jerusalem (Ἰερουσαλήμ καινή, Ierousalēm kainē, Strong's G2419 & G2537): The holy city as the dwelling place of God's people.

- God's Presence (σκηνή, skēnē,

Strong's G4633): God dwelling with humanity.

Practical Applications:

- Anticipating Eternity: Living with a focus on the eternal kingdom.

- Embracing God's Presence: Seeking a deeper relationship with God in anticipation of His eternal presence.

The Implications for Believers

Living in Expectation

Believers are called to live in constant expectation of Christ's return, maintaining vigilance and faithfulness.

1 Thessalonians 5:1-6:

"But of the times and the seasons, brethren, ye have no need that I write unto you. For yourselves know perfectly that the day of the Lord so cometh as a thief in the night. For when they shall say, Peace and safety; then sudden destruction cometh upon them, as travail upon a woman with child; and they shall not escape. But ye, brethren, are not in darkness, that that day should overtake you as a thief. Ye are all the children of light, and the children of the day: we are not of the night, nor of darkness. Therefore let us not sleep, as do others; but let us watch and be sober."

Key Elements:

- Day of the Lord (ἡμέρα κυρίου, hēmera kyriou, Strong's G2250 & G2962): The time of Christ's return.

- Children of Light (υἱὸς τοῦ φωτός, huios tou phōtos, Strong's G5207 & G5457): Believers as those who live in God's light.

- Watchfulness (γρηγορέω, grēgoreō, Strong's G1127): The call to be alert and vigilant.

Practical Applications:

- Staying Vigilant: Being spiritually awake and prepared for Christ's return.

- Living in Light: Reflecting the values of God's kingdom in daily life.

Encouraging One Another

Believers are encouraged to comfort and build each other up with the hope of Christ's return.

1 Thessalonians 4:16-18:

"For the Lord himself shall descend from heaven with a shout, with the voice of the archangel, and with the trump of God: and the dead in Christ shall rise first: Then we which are alive and remain shall be caught up together with them in the clouds, to meet the Lord in the air: and so shall we ever be with the Lord. Wherefore comfort one another with these words."

Key Elements:

- Descent of the Lord (καταβαίνω, katabainō, Strong's G2597): Jesus' return from heaven.

- Resurrection of the Dead (ἀνάστασις νεκρῶν, anastasis nekrōn, Strong's G386 & G3498): The resurrection of believers.

- Eternal Reunion (πάντοτε σὺν κυρίῳ, pantote syn kyriō, Strong's G3842 & G4862 & G2962): Being with the Lord forever.

Practical Applications:

- Encouraging Others: Offering hope and comfort to fellow believers with the promise of Christ's return.

- Building Community: Strengthening the church through mutual support and encouragement.

Living Holy and Godly Lives

The expectation of Christ's return motivates believers to pursue holiness and godliness.

2 Peter 3:10-14:

"But the day of the Lord will come as a thief in the night; in the which the heavens shall pass away with a great noise, and the elements shall melt with fervent heat, the earth also and the works that are therein shall be burned up. Seeing then that all these things shall be dissolved, what manner of persons ought ye to be in all holy conversation and godliness, Looking for and hasting unto the coming of the day of God, wherein the heavens being on fire shall be dissolved, and the elements shall melt with fervent heat? Nevertheless we, according to his promise, look for new heavens and a new earth, wherein dwelleth righteousness. Wherefore, beloved, seeing that ye look for such things, be diligent that ye may be found of him in peace, without spot, and blameless."

Key Elements:

- Day of the Lord: The time of final judgment and renewal.

- Holy and Godly Lives (ἀναστροφή ἅγιος καὶ εὐσέβεια, anastrophē hagios kai eusebeia, Strong's G391 & G40 & G2150): Conduct reflecting God's character.

Practical Applications:

- Pursuing Holiness: Striving to live in a way that honors God.

- Anticipating Renewal: Living with the hope of the new heavens and new earth.

The return of Christ is the culmination of God's redemptive plan, bringing ultimate victory over evil, the fulfillment of all prophecy, and the establishment of God's eternal kingdom. This event is central to Christian hope and motivates believers to live in a manner worthy of their calling. By understanding the biblical foundations of the Second Coming, recognizing its significance, and embracing its implications for daily life, believers can live with confidence, purpose, and anticipation of the glorious future that awaits.

As we look forward to the return of our Lord, let us remain vigilant, encourage one another, and pursue holiness, knowing that our labor in the Lord is not in vain and that His promises are sure. The Second Coming of Christ offers a beacon of hope, guiding us through the complexities of life and assuring us of God's ultimate victory and eternal reign.

Hope and Preparation for Believers

The hope of Christ's return is a central tenet of the Christian faith, offering believers a source of profound encouragement and motivation. This hope is not merely passive but calls for active preparation, living in a manner that reflects the values and expectations of God's Kingdom. In this chapter, we will explore the nature of this hope, its implications for daily living, and the practical steps believers can take to prepare for the return of Christ. We will use Bible verses, expository study, and insights from Strong's Concordance to provide a comprehensive understanding of hope and preparation for believers.

The Nature of Christian Hope

The Assurance of Christ's Return

The return of Christ is a guaranteed event, as assured by Jesus Himself and echoed throughout the New Testament.

John 14:1-3:

"Let not your heart be troubled: ye believe in God, believe also in me. In my Father's house are many mansions: if it were not so, I would have told you. I go to prepare a place for you. And if I go and prepare a place for you, I will come again, and receive you unto myself; that where I am, there ye may be also."

Key Elements:

- Assurance of Return (ἔρχομαι, erchomai, Strong's G2064): Jesus' promise to come again.

- Eternal Dwelling: The place prepared for believers in the Father's house.

Practical Applications:

- Trusting in Jesus' Promise: Relying on the certainty of Christ's return.

- Living with Assurance: Allowing the promise of Christ's return to influence daily decisions and attitudes.

The Living Hope

Peter describes the hope of believers as a "living hope," grounded in the resurrection of Jesus Christ.

1 Peter 1:3-4:

"Blessed be the God and Father of our Lord Jesus Christ, which according to his abundant mercy hath begotten us again unto a lively hope by the resurrection of Jesus Christ from the dead, To an inheritance incorruptible, and undefiled, and that fadeth not away, reserved in heaven for you."

Key Elements:

- Living Hope (ζῶσα ἐλπίς, zōsa elpis, Strong's G2198 & G1680): A dynamic and enduring hope.

- Inheritance (κληρονομία, klēronomia, Strong's G2817): The eternal inheritance reserved for believers.

Practical Applications:

- Embracing Hope: Living with a confident expectation of future glory.

- Focusing on Eternal Inheritance: Prioritizing eternal values over temporal concerns.

The Implications of Hope for Daily Living

Encouragement in Suffering

The hope of Christ's return provides comfort and encouragement in the midst of trials and suffering.

Romans 8:18:

"For I reckon that the sufferings of this present time are not worthy to be compared with the glory which shall be revealed in us."

Key Elements:

- Present Sufferings (πάθημα, pathēma, Strong's G3804): The temporary hardships faced by believers.

- Future Glory (δόξα, doxa, Strong's G1391): The eternal glory that awaits believers.

Practical Applications:

- Enduring Suffering with Hope: Finding strength in the promise of future glory.

- Maintaining Perspective: Viewing current trials in light of eternal rewards.

Motivation for Holiness

The anticipation of Christ's return motivates believers to pursue holiness and godliness.

1 John 3:2-3:

"Beloved, now are we the sons of God, and it doth not yet appear what we shall be: but we know that, when he shall appear, we shall be like him; for we shall see him as he is. And every man that hath this hope in him purifieth himself, even as he is pure."

Key Elements:

- Transformation at His Coming: Believers will be transformed to be like Christ.

- Pursuit of Purity (ἁγνίζω, hagnizō, Strong's G48): The call to live pure and holy lives.

Practical Applications:

- Striving for Purity: Actively seeking to live a life that reflects the holiness of Christ.

- Preparing for Transformation: Allowing the hope of becoming like Christ to shape daily conduct.

Encouraging One Another

Believers are called to encourage one another with the hope of Christ's return, building each other up in faith and love.

1 Thessalonians 4:16-18:

"For the Lord himself shall descend from heaven with a shout, with the voice of the archangel, and with the trump of God: and the dead in Christ shall rise first: Then we which are alive and remain shall be caught up together with them in the clouds, to meet the Lord in the air: and so shall we ever be with the Lord. Wherefore comfort one another with these words."

Key Elements:

- The Return of Christ: The detailed description of Jesus' return and the resurrection of believers.

- Comfort One Another (παρακαλέω, parakaleō, Strong's G3870): The call to encourage and comfort fellow believers.

Practical Applications:

- Offering Encouragement: Using the promise of Christ's return to comfort and strengthen others.

- Building Community: Fostering a supportive and encouraging faith community.

Practical Steps for Preparation

Spiritual Vigilance

Believers are exhorted to remain vigilant, watching and praying for the return of Christ.

Matthew 24:42-44:

"Watch therefore: for ye know not what hour your Lord doth come. But know this, that if the goodman of the house had known in what watch the thief would come, he would have watched, and would not have suffered his house to be broken up. Therefore be ye also ready: for in such an hour as ye think not the Son of man cometh."

Key Elements:

- Watchfulness (γρηγορέω, grēgoreō, Strong's G1127): Staying alert and prepared for Christ's return.

- Readiness (ἕτοιμος, hetoimos, Strong's G2092): Being prepared for the unexpected timing of Jesus' return.

Practical Applications:

- Maintaining Spiritual Vigilance: Regularly engaging in prayer, Bible study, and worship.

- Living Prepared: Cultivating a lifestyle of readiness for Christ's return.

Active Service

Believers are called to actively serve others, using their gifts and talents to advance God's Kingdom.

Matthew 25:14-30 (Parable of the Talents):

"For the kingdom of heaven is as a man travelling into a far country, who called his own servants, and delivered unto them his goods. And unto one he gave five talents, to another two, and to another one; to every man according to his several ability; and straightway took his journey. Then he that had received the five talents went and traded with the same, and made them other five talents. And likewise he that had received two, he also gained other two. But he that had received one went and digged in the earth, and hid his lord's money. After a long time the lord of those servants cometh, and reckoneth with them. And so he that had received five talents came and brought other five talents, saying, Lord, thou deliveredst unto me five talents: behold, I have gained beside them five talents more. His lord said unto him, Well done, thou good and faithful servant: thou hast been faithful over a few things, I will make thee ruler over many things: enter thou into the joy of thy lord. He also that had received two talents came and said, Lord, thou deliveredst unto me two talents: behold, I have gained two other talents beside them. His lord said unto him, Well done, good and faithful servant; thou hast been faithful over a few things, I will make thee ruler over many things: enter thou into the joy of thy lord. Then he which had received the one talent came and said, Lord, I knew thee that thou art an hard man, reaping where thou hast not sown, and gathering where thou hast not strawed: And I was afraid, and went and hid thy talent in the earth: lo, there thou hast that is thine. His lord answered and said unto him, Thou wicked and slothful servant, thou knewest that I reap where I sowed not, and gather where I have not strawed: Thou oughtest therefore to have put my money to the exchangers, and then at my coming I should have received mine own with usury. Take therefore the talent from him, and give it unto him which hath ten talents. For unto every one that hath shall be given, and he shall have abundance: but from him that hath not shall be taken away even that which he hath. And cast ye the unprofitable servant into outer darkness: there shall be weeping and gnashing of teeth."

Key Elements:

- Use of Talents (τάλαντον, talanton, Strong's G5007): Utilizing gifts and resources for God's purposes.

- Faithful Service (πιστός, pistos, Strong's G4103): Being diligent and faithful in serving God.

Practical Applications:

- Serving Faithfully: Actively using one's gifts and talents to serve others and advance the Kingdom.

- Maximizing Opportunities: Being proactive in seeking ways to contribute to God's work.

Maintaining Holiness

Believers are called to live holy and godly lives, reflecting the character of Christ as they await His return.

2 Peter 3:11-14:

"Seeing then that all these things shall be dissolved, what manner of persons ought ye to be in all holy conversation and godliness, Looking for and hasting unto the coming of the day of God, wherein the heavens being on fire shall be dissolved, and the elements shall melt with fervent heat? Nevertheless we, according to his promise, look for new heavens and a new earth, wherein dwelleth righteousness. Wherefore, beloved, seeing that ye look for such things, be diligent that ye may be found of him in peace, without spot, and blameless."

Key Elements:

- Holy Conduct (ἅγιος ἀναστροφή, hagios anastrophē, Strong's G40 & G391): Living a life that is set apart for God.

- Diligence in Godliness (σπουδάζω, spoudazō, Strong's G4704): Making every effort to live a godly life.

Practical Applications:

- Pursuing Holiness: Striving to live in a way that honors God and reflects His holiness.

- Being Blameless: Maintaining integrity and moral purity in all aspects of life.

Encouraging One Another

Believers are exhorted to encourage and build each other up as they await the return of Christ.

Hebrews 10:24-25:

"And let us consider one another to provoke unto love and to good works: Not forsaking the assembling of ourselves together, as the manner of some is; but exhorting one another: and so much the more, as ye see the day approaching."

Key Elements:

- Provoking to Love and Good Works (παροξυσμός, paroxysmos, Strong's G3948 & ἔργον, ergon, Strong's G2041): Encouraging each other to live out love and good deeds.

- Exhorting One Another (παρακαλέω, parakaleō, Strong's G3870): Offering encouragement and support within the community of believers.

Practical Applications:

- Fostering Community: Regularly gathering with other believers for mutual encouragement and support.

- Encouraging Growth: Inspiring others to pursue love, good works, and spiritual growth.

The hope of Christ's return is a powerful motivator for believers, inspiring them to live in a manner that honors God and reflects the values of His Kingdom. This hope provides encouragement in times of suffering, motivates the pursuit of holiness, and calls believers to actively serve others and build one another up.

By maintaining spiritual vigilance, using their gifts to serve, pursuing holiness, and encouraging one another, believers can prepare for the return of Christ with confidence and joy. The promise of His return offers a beacon of hope, guiding believers through the complexities of life and assuring them of the ultimate fulfillment of God's redemptive plan. As we live in anticipation of this glorious event, let us remain faithful, diligent, and hopeful, knowing that our labor in the Lord is not in vain and that His promises are sure.

CHAPTER 10

JESUS AS THE SAVIOR

Summarizing the Prophecies and Their Fulfillment in Christ

The identity of Jesus as the Savior is the cornerstone of the Christian faith. Throughout the Old and New Testaments, numerous prophecies foreshadow and detail the coming of the Messiah, who would bring salvation to humanity. In this chapter, we will summarize these prophecies and explore how they find their fulfillment in the life, death, and resurrection of Jesus Christ. By examining the biblical evidence and its theological implications, we will gain a deeper understanding of Jesus' role as the Savior of the world.

Old Testament Prophecies of the Messiah

The Seed of the Woman

The first prophecy regarding the coming Savior is found in Genesis, where God promises a deliverer who will crush the serpent's head.

Genesis 3:15:

"And I will put enmity between thee and the woman, and between thy seed and her seed; it shall bruise thy head, and thou shalt bruise his heel."

Key Elements:

- Seed of the Woman (זֶרַע, zera, Strong's H2233): Refers to a descendant of Eve who will defeat Satan.

- Bruise the Head: Signifies a mortal blow to the serpent, symbolizing Satan.

Fulfillment in Christ:

- Galatians 4:4-5: "But when the fulness of the time was come, God sent forth his Son, made of a woman, made under the law, To redeem them that were under the law, that we might receive the adoption of sons."

Practical Applications:

- Recognizing Jesus as the Fulfillment: Understanding that Jesus' victory over sin and Satan fulfills this ancient promise.

- Living in Victory: Embracing the victory over sin that Jesus secured.

The Promise to Abraham

God's promise to Abraham included the assurance that through his offspring, all nations would be blessed.

Genesis 12:3:

"And I will bless them that bless thee, and curse him that curseth thee: and in thee shall all families of the earth be blessed."

Key Elements:

- Blessing to All Nations (בָּרַךְ, barak, Strong's H1288): The global impact of Abraham's descendant.

Fulfillment in Christ:

- Galatians 3:8: "And the scripture, foreseeing that God would justify the heathen through faith, preached before the gospel unto Abraham, saying, In thee shall all nations be blessed."

Practical Applications:

- Understanding Universal Blessing: Recognizing Jesus as the fulfillment of the promise to bless all nations.

- Sharing the Gospel: Participating in the global mission to spread the blessings of Christ.

The Prophecy of the Suffering Servant

Isaiah's prophecy of the suffering servant vividly describes the Messiah's sacrificial role in bearing the sins of humanity.

Isaiah 53:3-7:

"He is despised and rejected of men; a man of sorrows, and acquainted with grief: and we hid as it were our faces from him; he was despised, and we esteemed him not. Surely he hath borne our griefs, and carried our sorrows: yet we did esteem him stricken, smitten of God, and afflicted. But he was wounded for our transgressions, he was bruised for our iniquities: the chastisement of our peace was upon him; and with his stripes we are healed. All we like sheep have gone astray; we have turned every one to his own way; and the Lord hath laid on him the iniquity of us all. He was oppressed, and he was afflicted, yet he opened not his mouth: he is brought as a lamb to the slaughter, and as a sheep before her shearers is dumb, so he openeth not his mouth."

Key Elements:

- Man of Sorrows (מַכְאוֹבוֹת אִישׁ, ish makovot, Strong's H376 & H4341): The suffering and rejection of the Messiah.

- Borne Our Griefs: The Messiah's sacrificial bearing of humanity's sins.

Fulfillment in Christ:

- 1 Peter 2:24: "Who his own self bare our sins in his own body on the tree, that we, being dead to sins, should live unto righteousness: by whose stripes ye were healed."

Practical Applications:

- Acknowledging Jesus' Sacrifice: Understanding the depth of Jesus' suffering for our sins.

- Living in Gratitude: Responding to Jesus' sacrifice with gratitude and devotion.

The Promise of a New Covenant

Jeremiah prophesied a new covenant that God would establish with His people, characterized by an internal transformation and forgiveness of sins.

Jeremiah 31:31-34:

"Behold, the days come, saith the Lord, that I will make a new covenant with the house of Israel, and with the house of Judah: Not according to the covenant that I made with their fathers in the day that I took them by the hand to bring them out of the land of Egypt; which my covenant they brake, although I was an husband unto them, saith the Lord: But this shall be the covenant that I will make with the house of Israel; After those days, saith the Lord, I will put my law in their inward parts, and write it in their hearts; and will be their God, and they shall be my people. And they shall teach no more every man his neighbour, and every man his brother, saying, Know the Lord: for they shall all know me, from the least of them unto the greatest of them, saith the Lord: for I will forgive their iniquity, and I will remember their sin no more."

Key Elements:

- New Covenant (חֲדָשָׁה בְּרִית, berit chadashah, Strong's H1285 & H2319): A renewed relationship between God and His people.

- Internal Transformation: God's law written on hearts.

Fulfillment in Christ:

- Luke 22:20: "Likewise also the cup after supper, saying, This cup is the new testament in my blood, which is shed for you."

Practical Applications:

- Embracing the New Covenant: Living in the reality of the new covenant established by Jesus' sacrifice.

- Seeking Internal Transformation: Allowing the Holy Spirit to write God's laws on our hearts.

New Testament Fulfillment of Messianic Prophecies

The Birth of Jesus

The New Testament records the fulfillment of Old Testament prophecies concerning the birth of the Messiah.

Isaiah 7:14:

"Therefore the Lord himself shall give you a sign; Behold, a virgin shall conceive, and bear a son, and shall call his name Immanuel."

Fulfillment in Christ:

- Matthew 1:22-23: "Now all this was done, that it might be fulfilled which was spoken of the Lord by the prophet, saying, Behold, a virgin shall be with child, and shall bring forth a son, and they shall call his name Emmanuel, which being interpreted is, God with us."

Key Elements:

- Virgin Birth (παρθένος, parthenos, Strong's G3933): A miraculous birth fulfilling prophecy.

- Immanuel (אֵל עִמָּנוּ, Immanuel, Strong's H6005): Meaning "God with us."

Practical Applications:

- Acknowledging Jesus' Divinity: Recognizing Jesus as God incarnate.

- Celebrating the Incarnation: Reflecting on the miracle of Jesus' birth and its significance.

The Ministry of Jesus

The life and ministry of Jesus fulfilled numerous Old Testament prophecies, demonstrating His identity as the Messiah.

Isaiah 61:1-2:

"The Spirit of the Lord God is upon me; because the Lord hath anointed me to preach good tidings unto the meek; he hath sent me to bind up the brokenhearted, to proclaim liberty to the captives, and the opening of the prison to them that are bound; To proclaim the acceptable year of the Lord, and the day of vengeance of our God; to comfort all that mourn;"

Fulfillment in Christ:

- Luke 4:16-21: "And he came to Nazareth, where he had been brought up: and, as his custom was, he went into the synagogue on the sabbath day, and stood up for to read. And there was delivered unto him the book of the prophet Esaias. And when he had opened the book, he found the place where it was written, The Spirit of the Lord is upon me, because he hath anointed me to preach the gospel to the poor; he hath sent me to heal the brokenhearted, to preach deliverance to the captives, and recovering of sight to the blind, to set at liberty them that are bruised, To preach the acceptable year of the Lord. And he closed the book, and he gave it again to the minister, and sat down. And the eyes of all them that were in the synagogue were fastened on him. And he began to say unto them, This day is this scripture fulfilled in your ears."

Key Elements:

- Preaching Good Tidings (εὐαγγελίζω, euangelizō, Strong's G2097): Proclaiming the gospel.

- Healing and Deliverance: Jesus' ministry of compassion and liberation.

Practical Applications:

- Following Jesus' Example: Engaging in ministries of compassion, healing, and liberation.

- Proclaiming the Gospel: Sharing the good news of Jesus Christ with others.

The Death and Resurrection of Jesus

The death and resurrection of Jesus are the ultimate fulfillment of Old Testament sacrificial themes and the cornerstone of salvation.

Psalm 22:16-18:

"For dogs have compassed me: the assembly of the wicked have inclosed me: they pierced my hands and my feet. I may tell all my bones: they look and stare upon me. They part my garments among them, and cast lots upon my vesture."

Fulfillment in Christ:

- John 19:23-24: "Then the soldiers, when they had crucified Jesus, took his garments, and made four parts, to every soldier a part; and also his coat: now the coat was without seam, woven from the top throughout. They said therefore among themselves, Let us not rend it, but cast lots for it, whose it shall be: that the scripture might be fulfilled, which saith, They parted my raiment among them, and for my vesture they did cast lots. These things therefore the soldiers did."

Key Elements:

- Crucifixion (σταυρόω, stauroō, Strong's G4717): The specific details of Jesus' suffering and death.

- Resurrection: The victory over death and the validation of Jesus' divine mission.

Practical Applications:

- Trusting in Jesus' Sacrifice: Believing in the atoning work of Jesus on the cross.

- Living in Resurrection Power: Embracing the new life and victory available through Jesus' resurrection.

The Theological Significance of Jesus as the Savior

The Atonement for Sin

Jesus' death on the cross provides the atonement for humanity's sins, fulfilling the sacrificial system of the Old Testament.

Romans 3:25-26:

"Whom God hath set forth to be a propitiation through faith in his blood, to declare his righteousness for the remission of sins that are past, through the forbearance of God; To declare, I say, at this time his righteousness: that he might be just, and the justifier of him which believeth in Jesus."

Key Elements:

- Propitiation (ἱλαστήριον, hilastērion, Strong's G2435): The satisfaction of God's wrath through Jesus' sacrifice.

- Justification (δικαιόω, dikaioō, Strong's G1344): Being declared righteous through faith in Jesus.

Practical Applications:

- Receiving Forgiveness: Embracing the forgiveness and justification offered through Jesus.

- Living in Righteousness: Walking in the new identity as justified believers.

The Defeat of Death

Jesus' resurrection signifies the defeat of death and the promise of eternal life for believers.

1 Corinthians 15:54-57:

"So when this corruptible shall have put on incorruption, and this mortal shall have put on immortality, then shall be brought to pass the saying that is written, Death is swallowed up in victory. O death, where is thy sting? O grave, where is thy victory? The sting of death is sin; and the strength of sin is the law. But thanks be to God, which giveth us the victory through our Lord Jesus Christ."

Key Elements:

- Victory Over Death (νῖκος, nikos, Strong's G3534): The triumph over death through Jesus' resurrection.

- Eternal Life: The promise of immortality for believers.

Practical Applications:

- Living with Hope: Embracing the hope of eternal life and victory over death.

- Sharing the Good News: Proclaiming the message of resurrection and eternal life to others.

The Restoration of Relationship with God

Through Jesus, believers are reconciled to God and restored to a right relationship with Him.

2 Corinthians 5:18-19:

"And all things are of God, who hath reconciled us to himself by Jesus Christ, and hath given to us the ministry of reconciliation; To wit, that God was in Christ, reconciling the world unto himself, not imputing their trespasses unto them; and hath committed unto us the word of reconciliation."

Key Elements:

- Reconciliation (καταλλάσσω, katallassō, Strong's G2644): Restoring a broken relationship.

- Ministry of Reconciliation: The call to share the message of reconciliation with others.

Practical Applications:

- Embracing Reconciliation: Living in the restored relationship with God through Jesus.

- Engaging in Reconciliation: Actively participating in the ministry of reconciliation, sharing the message of God's grace and forgiveness.

The prophecies of the Old Testament find their ultimate fulfillment in Jesus Christ, who is the promised Savior. From His birth to His ministry, death, and resurrection, Jesus fulfills every detail foretold by the prophets, affirming His identity as the Messiah. The theological significance of Jesus as the Savior encompasses atonement for sin, victory over death, and the restoration of relationship with God.

As believers, we are called to live in the light of these fulfilled prophecies, embracing the salvation Jesus offers and sharing this good news with others. Understanding Jesus as the fulfillment of prophecy deepens our faith, strengthens our hope, and compels us to live lives that reflect the transformative power of the gospel. Through Jesus, we find not only the fulfillment of ancient promises but also the hope and assurance of eternal life with God.

Jesus' Role as the Savior of Humanity

The identity of Jesus Christ as the Savior of humanity is the cornerstone of Christian theology. His life, death, and resurrection constitute the pivotal events that offer redemption to all who believe. This chapter explores Jesus' role as the Savior, examining the biblical basis, theological significance, and practical implications for believers. We will delve into how Jesus fulfills the Messianic prophecies, the nature of His redemptive work, and the transformative impact of His salvation on humanity.

The Biblical Basis for Jesus as Savior

Old Testament Foundations

The Old Testament lays the groundwork for understanding the coming of the Savior through various prophecies and types.

Genesis 3:15:

"And I will put enmity between thee and the woman, and between thy seed and her seed; it shall bruise thy head, and thou shalt bruise his heel."

Key Elements:

- Protoevangelium: The first gospel proclamation, indicating a future victory over sin and Satan by the seed of the woman.

Isaiah 53:4-5:

"Surely he hath borne our griefs, and carried our sorrows: yet we did esteem him stricken, smitten of God, and afflicted. But he was wounded for our transgressions, he was bruised for our iniquities: the chastisement of our peace was upon him; and with his stripes we are healed."

Key Elements:

- Suffering Servant: A prophetic picture of the Messiah bearing the sins of humanity.

New Testament Fulfillment

The New Testament unequivocally presents Jesus as the fulfillment of these prophecies and the Savior of the world.

Matthew 1:21:

"And she shall bring forth a son, and thou shalt call his name JESUS: for he shall save his people from their sins."

Key Elements:

- Name of Jesus (Ἰησοῦς, Iēsous, Strong's G2424): Meaning "The Lord saves," directly linking Jesus to His saving work.

John 1:29:

"The next day John seeth Jesus coming unto him, and saith, Behold the Lamb of God, which taketh away the sin of the world."

Key Elements:

- Lamb of God: A reference to the sacrificial system, indicating Jesus' role as the ultimate sacrifice for sin.

Romans 5:8:

"But God commendeth his love toward us, in that, while we were yet sinners, Christ died for us."

Key Elements:

- Demonstration of Love: Jesus' sacrificial death as the ultimate expression of God's love for humanity.

The Nature of Jesus' Redemptive Work

Atonement for Sin

Jesus' death on the cross provides atonement for sin, satisfying the requirements of divine justice.

Hebrews 9:26:

"For then must he often have suffered since the foundation of the world: but now once in the end of the world hath he appeared to put away sin by the sacrifice of himself."

Key Elements:

- Once for All Sacrifice: The final and sufficient sacrifice for sin.

1 John 2:2:

"And he is the propitiation for our sins: and not for ours only, but also for the sins of the whole world."

Key Elements:

- Propitiation (ἱλασμός, hilasmos, Strong's G2434): The appeasement of God's wrath through Jesus' sacrifice.

Victory Over Death

Jesus' resurrection signifies His victory over death, offering believers the hope of eternal life.

1 Corinthians 15:20-22:

"But now is Christ risen from the dead, and become the firstfruits of them that slept. For since by man came death, by man came also the resurrection of the dead. For as in Adam all die, even so in Christ shall all be made alive."

Key Elements:

- Firstfruits: Jesus' resurrection as the guarantee of believers' future resurrection.

Revelation 1:18:

"I am he that liveth, and was dead; and, behold, I am alive for evermore, Amen; and have the keys of hell and of death."

Key Elements:

- Keys of Death and Hades: Jesus' authority over death and the grave.

Reconciliation with God

Jesus' work reconciles humanity to God, restoring the broken relationship caused by sin.

2 Corinthians 5:18-19:

"And all things are of God, who hath reconciled us to himself by Jesus Christ, and hath given to us the ministry of reconciliation; To wit, that God was in Christ, reconciling the world unto himself, not imputing their trespasses unto them; and hath committed unto us the word of reconciliation."

Key Elements:

- Ministry of Reconciliation (καταλλαγή, katallagē, Strong's G2643): The restoration of fellowship between God and humanity through Jesus.

The Transformative Impact of Jesus' Salvation

New Identity in Christ

Believers are given a new identity in Christ, characterized by righteousness and holiness.

2 Corinthians 5:17:

"Therefore if any man be in Christ, he is a new creature: old things are passed away; behold, all things are become new."

Key Elements:

- New Creation (καινὴ κτίσις, kainē ktisis, Strong's G2537 & G2937): The transformative effect of salvation on the believer's life.

Ephesians 4:24:

"And that ye put on the new man, which after God is created in righteousness and true holiness."

Key Elements:

- New Self: The renewal of the believer's nature in righteousness and holiness.

Freedom from Sin

Jesus' salvation liberates believers from the power and penalty of sin, enabling them to live in freedom.

Romans 6:6-7:

"Knowing this, that our old man is crucified with him, that the body of sin might be destroyed, that henceforth we should not serve sin. For he that is dead is freed from sin."

Key Elements:

- Freedom from Sin (ἐλευθερόω, eleutheroō, Strong's G1659): Liberation from the dominion of sin.

Galatians 5:1:

"Stand fast therefore in the liberty wherewith Christ hath made us free, and be not entangled again with the yoke of bondage."

Key Elements:

- Liberty in Christ (ἐλευθερία, eleutheria, Strong's G1657): The freedom that believers have in Christ.

Eternal Life

Jesus' role as Savior guarantees eternal life to those who believe in Him, offering a hope that transcends this life.

John 3:16:

"For God so loved the world, that he gave his only begotten Son, that whosoever believeth in him should not perish, but have everlasting life."

Key Elements:

- Eternal Life (αἰώνιος ζωή, aiōnios zōē, Strong's G166 & G2222): The promise of life that never ends for believers.

1 John 5:11-12:

"And this is the record, that God hath given to us eternal life, and this life is in his Son. He that hath the Son hath life; and he that hath not the Son of God hath not life."

Key Elements:

- Life in the Son: Eternal life is found in a relationship with Jesus.

The Practical Implications for Believers

Living in Gratitude

Believers are called to live lives of gratitude, continually thanking God for the gift of salvation through Jesus.

Colossians 3:15-17:

"And let the peace of God rule in your hearts, to the which also ye are called in one body; and be ye thankful. Let the word of Christ dwell in you richly in all wisdom; teaching and admonishing one another in psalms and hymns and spiritual songs, singing with grace in your hearts to the Lord. And whatsoever ye do in word or deed, do all in the name of the Lord Jesus, giving thanks to God and the Father by him."

Key Elements:

- Thankfulness (εὐχαριστέω, eucharisteō, Strong's G2168): A continual attitude of gratitude for God's grace.

Practical Applications:

- Expressing Gratitude: Regularly thanking God in prayer, worship, and daily living.

- Cultivating a Grateful Heart: Developing an attitude of thankfulness in all circumstances.

Proclaiming the Gospel

Believers are entrusted with the responsibility of sharing the good news of Jesus' salvation with others.

Matthew 28:19-20:

"Go ye therefore, and teach all nations, baptizing them in the name of the Father, and of the Son, and of the Holy Ghost: Teaching them to observe all things whatsoever I have commanded you: and, lo, I am with you alway, even unto the end of the world. Amen."

Key Elements:

- Great Commission (ἐξουσία, exousia, Strong's G1849): The authority and mandate to make disciples.

Acts 1:8:

"But ye shall receive power, after that the Holy Ghost is come upon you: and ye shall be witnesses unto me both in Jerusalem, and in all Judaea, and in Samaria, and unto the uttermost part of the earth."

Key Elements:

Witnesses (μάρτυς, martys, Strong's G3144): Believers are called to testify to the truth of Jesus.

Practical Applications:

- Evangelism: Actively sharing the gospel with others through words and actions.

- Living as Witnesses: Demonstrating the transformative power of Jesus in daily life.

Living in Hope

The hope of eternal life and the return of Christ provides a foundation for living with purpose and anticipation.

Titus 2:13-14:

"Looking for that blessed hope, and the glorious appearing of the great God and our Saviour Jesus Christ; Who gave himself for us, that he might redeem us from all iniquity, and purify unto himself a peculiar people, zealous of good works."

Key Elements:

- Blessed Hope (μακαρία ἐλπίς, makaria elpis, Strong's G3107 & G1680): The confident expectation of Christ's return and the fulfillment of His promises.

1 Peter 1:3-5:

"Blessed be the God and Father of our Lord Jesus Christ, which according to his abundant mercy hath begotten us again unto a lively hope by the resurrection of Jesus Christ from the dead, To an inheritance incorruptible, and undefiled, and that fadeth not away, reserved in heaven for you, Who are kept by the power of God through faith unto salvation ready to be revealed in the last time."

Key Elements:

- Living Hope (ζῶσα ἐλπίς, zōsa elpis, Strong's G2198 & G1680): The dynamic and enduring hope grounded in Jesus' resurrection.

Practical Applications:

- Living with Anticipation: Fostering an attitude of expectation for Christ's return.

- Finding Strength in Hope: Drawing encouragement and motivation from the hope of eternal life.

Jesus' role as the Savior of humanity is the central theme of the Christian faith, encompassing His fulfillment of Old Testament prophecies, His redemptive work on the cross, and His resurrection. This role carries profound theological significance, offering atonement for sin, victory over death, and reconciliation with God. For believers, understanding and embracing Jesus as the Savior transforms their identity, liberates them from sin, and provides the hope of eternal life.

Living in response to Jesus' salvation involves a life of gratitude, active proclamation of the gospel, and living with hope and purpose. As we reflect on Jesus' role as the Savior, let us be continually thankful, share the good news with others, and live in the confident expectation of His return, knowing that through Him, we have received the greatest gift of all—eternal life and a restored relationship with God.

The Significance of His Sacrifice and Resurrection

The sacrifice and resurrection of Jesus Christ are the cornerstone of the Christian faith, representing the culmination of God's redemptive plan for humanity. These events are not merely historical occurrences but carry profound theological significance, transforming the lives of believers and offering hope for eternal life. In this chapter, we will explore the significance of Jesus' sacrifice and resurrection, examining the biblical basis, theological implications, and practical applications for believers.

The Sacrifice of Jesus

The Necessity of the Sacrifice

The sacrificial death of Jesus was necessary to fulfill the requirements of divine justice and to atone for the sins of humanity.

Romans 3:23-25:

"For all have sinned, and come short of the glory of God; Being justified freely by his grace through the redemption that is in Christ Jesus: Whom God hath set forth to be a propitiation through faith in his blood, to declare his righteousness for the remission of sins that are past, through the forbearance of God."

Key Elements:

- Universal Sin (ἁμαρτία, hamartia, Strong's G266): The sinful nature of all humanity.

- Propitiation (ἱλαστήριον, hilastērion, Strong's G2435): The appeasement of God's wrath through Jesus' blood.

Practical Applications:

- Acknowledging Sin: Recognizing the universal need for redemption.

- Embracing Atonement: Accepting Jesus' sacrifice as the means of reconciliation with God.

The Fulfillment of Prophecy

Jesus' sacrificial death was foretold in the Old Testament, fulfilling Messianic prophecies and demonstrating the continuity of God's plan.

Isaiah 53:5-6:

"But he was wounded for our transgressions, he was bruised for our iniquities: the chastisement of our peace was upon him; and with his stripes we are healed. All we like sheep have gone astray; we have turned every one to his own way; and the Lord hath laid on him the iniquity of us all."

Key Elements:

- Wounded for Our Transgressions: The Messiah's suffering for the sins of humanity.

- Healing Through Stripes: The redemptive suffering of Jesus.

Practical Applications:

- Recognizing Fulfillment: Seeing Jesus as the fulfillment of Old Testament prophecies.

- Living in Gratitude: Responding with thankfulness for Jesus' sacrificial love.

The Perfect Sacrifice

Jesus' death on the cross was the perfect and final sacrifice, accomplishing what the Old Testament sacrificial system could only foreshadow.

Hebrews 10:10-12:

"By the which will we are sanctified through the offering of the body of Jesus Christ once for all. And every priest standeth daily ministering and offering oftentimes the same sacrifices, which can never take away sins: But this man, after he had offered one sacrifice for sins for ever, sat down on the right hand of God."

Key Elements:

- Once for All Sacrifice (ἐφάπαξ, ephapax, Strong's G2178): The completeness and finality of Jesus' offering.

- Sanctification (ἁγιάζω, hagiazō, Strong's G37): The process of being made holy through Jesus' sacrifice.

Practical Applications:

- Trusting in the Final Sacrifice: Relying on Jesus' once-for-all offering for forgiveness and sanctification.

- Living in Holiness: Pursuing a holy life in response to Jesus' sacrifice.

The Resurrection of Jesus

The Historical Reality

The resurrection of Jesus is a historical event attested by multiple witnesses and serves as the foundation of Christian faith.

1 Corinthians 15:3-8:

"For I delivered unto you first of all that which I also received, how that Christ died for our sins according to the scriptures; And that he was buried, and that he rose again the third day according to the scriptures: And that he was seen of Cephas, then of the twelve: After that, he was seen of above five hundred brethren at once; of whom the greater part remain unto this present, but some are fallen asleep. After that, he was seen of James; then of all the apostles. And last of all he was seen of me also, as of one born out of due time."

Key Elements:

- Eyewitness Testimony (μαρτυρία, martyria, Strong's G3141): The accounts of those who saw the risen Christ.

- Scriptural Fulfillment: The resurrection as fulfillment of Old Testament prophecies.

Practical Applications:

- Affirming the Resurrection: Believing in the historical reality of Jesus' resurrection.

- Sharing the Witness: Proclaiming the resurrection as a foundational truth of the gospel.

Theological Implications

The resurrection of Jesus has profound theological implications, affirming His divinity and guaranteeing the future resurrection of believers.

Romans 1:4:

"And declared to be the Son of God with power, according to the spirit of holiness, by the resurrection from the dead:"

Key Elements:

- Declaration of Divinity: The resurrection as proof of Jesus' divine nature.

1 Corinthians 15:20-22:

"But now is Christ risen from the dead, and become the firstfruits of them that slept. For since by man came death, by man came also the resurrection of the dead. For as in Adam all die, even so in Christ shall all be made alive."

Key Elements:

- Firstfruits (ἀπαρχή, aparchē, Strong's G536): Jesus' resurrection as the first of many to come.

- Future Resurrection: The promise of resurrection for all who are in Christ.

Practical Applications:

- Confessing Jesus as Lord: Recognizing the resurrection as the validation of Jesus' divinity and Lordship.

- Living in Hope: Embracing the promise of future resurrection and eternal life.

The Victory Over Death

The resurrection signifies Jesus' victory over death and the grave, offering believers hope and assurance of eternal life.

1 Corinthians 15:54-57:

"So when this corruptible shall have put on incorruption, and this mortal shall have put on immortality, then shall be brought to pass the saying that is written, Death is swallowed up in victory. O death, where is thy sting? O grave, where is thy victory? The sting of death is sin; and the strength of sin is the law. But thanks be to God, which giveth us the victory through our Lord Jesus Christ."

Key Elements:

- Victory Over Death (νῖκος, nikos, Strong's G3534): The defeat of death through Jesus' resurrection.

- Immortality (ἀθανασία, athanasia, Strong's G110): The promise of eternal life.

Practical Applications:

- Living in Victory: Embracing the victory over death that Jesus has secured.

- Facing Death with Hope: Approaching death with the assurance of eternal life in Christ.

The Practical Significance for Believers

A New Life in Christ

The resurrection of Jesus empowers believers to live a new life, characterized by righteousness and empowered by the Holy Spirit.

Romans 6:4:

"Therefore we are buried with him by baptism into death: that like as Christ was raised up from the dead by the glory of the Father, even so we also should walk in newness of life."

Key Elements:

- Newness of Life (καινότης ζωῆς, kainotēs zōēs, Strong's G2538 & G2222): The transformative impact of the resurrection on the believer's life.

2 Corinthians 5:17:

"Therefore if any man be in Christ, he is a new creature: old things are passed away; behold, all things are become new."

Key Elements:

- New Creation: The radical transformation of believers through their union with Christ.

Practical Applications:

- Living a Transformed Life: Walking in the new life that Jesus' resurrection makes possible.

- Embracing Change: Allowing the Holy Spirit to continually renew and transform us.

The Power of the Holy Spirit

The resurrection is closely linked with the outpouring of the Holy Spirit, who empowers believers for life and ministry.

Acts 2:32-33:

"This Jesus hath God raised up, whereof we all are witnesses. Therefore being by the right hand of God exalted, and having received of the Father the promise of the Holy Ghost, he hath shed forth this, which ye now see and hear."

Key Elements:

- Exaltation of Jesus: His ascension and the sending of the Holy Spirit.

- Promise of the Holy Spirit (ἐπαγγελία τοῦ πνεύματος, epangelia tou pneumatos, Strong's G1860 & G4151): The fulfillment of Jesus' promise to send the Holy Spirit.

Practical Applications:

- Seeking the Holy Spirit: Relying on the Holy Spirit for guidance, empowerment, and transformation.

- Living Spirit-Filled Lives: Allowing the Holy Spirit to work through us in everyday life and ministry.

Mission and Evangelism

The resurrection of Jesus compels believers to share the good news of the gospel with others, fulfilling the Great Commission.

Matthew 28:18-20:

"And Jesus came

 and spake unto them, saying, All power is given unto me in heaven and in earth. Go ye therefore, and teach all nations, baptizing them in the name of the Father, and of the Son, and of the Holy Ghost: Teaching them to observe all things whatsoever I have commanded you: and, lo, I am with you alway, even unto the end of the world. Amen."

Key Elements:

- Great Commission: The mandate to make disciples of all nations.

- Authority of Jesus (ἐξουσία, exousia, Strong's G1849): Jesus' authority as the risen Lord.

Acts 1:8:

"But ye shall receive power, after that the Holy Ghost is come upon you: and ye shall be witnesses unto me both in Jerusalem, and in all Judaea, and in Samaria, and unto the uttermost part of the earth."

Key Elements:

- Witnesses: Believers are called to testify to the reality of Jesus' resurrection.

Practical Applications:

- Engaging in Evangelism: Actively sharing the gospel with others.

- Making Disciples: Committing to disciple others and help them grow in their faith.

The sacrifice and resurrection of Jesus Christ are the pivotal events that offer salvation and hope to humanity. His sacrificial death fulfills the requirements of divine justice, atones for sin, and demonstrates God's immense love for us. His resurrection affirms His divinity, guarantees our future resurrection, and secures victory over death.

For believers, the significance of Jesus' sacrifice and resurrection is profound, transforming our identity, empowering us with the Holy Spirit, and compelling us to share the gospel. As we embrace the reality of Jesus' sacrifice and resurrection, let us live lives of gratitude, hope, and mission, fully devoted to the One who gave His life for us and conquered the grave.

CHAPTER 11

REFLECTION ON THE DIVINITY AND LESSONS OF JESUS CHRIST

As we conclude our exploration of Jesus Christ, we reflect on His divinity, the lessons He taught, and the profound impact His life, death, and resurrection have on humanity. Jesus is not only the fulfillment of ancient prophecies but also the living embodiment of God's love, grace, and truth. This chapter aims to encapsulate the significance of Jesus' divinity and teachings and to inspire believers to live in the light of His example and message.

The Divinity of Jesus Christ

Fulfillment of Prophecies

Jesus' life fulfilled numerous Old Testament prophecies, affirming His identity as the promised Messiah and the Son of God.

Isaiah 7:14:

"Therefore the Lord himself shall give you a sign; Behold, a virgin shall conceive, and bear a son, and shall call his name Immanuel."

Key Elements:

- Virgin Birth: Jesus' miraculous birth fulfilling prophecy.

- Immanuel: Meaning "God with us," signifying Jesus' divine nature.

Matthew 1:22-23:

"Now all this was done, that it might be fulfilled which was spoken of the Lord by the prophet, saying, Behold, a virgin shall be with child, and shall bring forth a son, and they shall call his name Emmanuel, which being interpreted is, God with us."

Practical Applications:

- Trust in Prophecy: Recognizing the fulfillment of prophecy in Jesus strengthens our faith in the reliability of Scripture.

- Acknowledging Jesus' Divinity: Embracing Jesus as God incarnate, who dwelt among us.

The Divine Nature of Jesus

Throughout His ministry, Jesus demonstrated His divine nature through His teachings, miracles, and authority.

John 1:1-3:

"In the beginning was the Word, and the Word was with God, and the Word was God. The same was in the beginning with God. All things were made by him; and without him was not any thing made that was made."

Key Elements:

- The Word: Identifies Jesus as the divine Logos, pre-existent and active in creation.

- Divine Authority: Jesus' authority over nature, sickness, and death confirms His divinity.

John 10:30:

"I and my Father are one."

Practical Applications:

- Worship and Reverence: Worshipping Jesus as divine and giving Him the reverence He deserves.

- Confidence in Jesus' Power: Trusting in His divine power in all aspects of life.

Lessons from the Life of Jesus

The Teachings of Jesus

Jesus' teachings provide profound insights into the nature of God, the kingdom of heaven, and the principles of righteous living.

Matthew 5:3-12 (The Beatitudes):

"Blessed are the poor in spirit: for theirs is the kingdom of heaven. Blessed are they that mourn: for they shall be comforted. Blessed are the meek: for they shall inherit the earth. Blessed are they which do hunger and thirst after righteousness: for they shall be filled. Blessed are the merciful: for they shall obtain mercy. Blessed are the pure in heart: for they shall see God. Blessed are the peacemakers: for they shall be called the children of God. Blessed are they which are persecuted for righteousness' sake: for theirs is the kingdom of heaven. Blessed are ye when men shall revile you, and persecute you, and shall say all manner of evil against you falsely, for my sake. Rejoice, and be exceeding glad: for great is your reward in heaven: for so persecuted they the prophets which were before you."

Key Elements:

- Kingdom Values: The Beatitudes outline the attitudes and behaviors that characterize citizens of God's kingdom.

- Righteous Living: Emphasizing humility, mercy, purity, and peacemaking.

Practical Applications:

- Embodying Kingdom Values: Striving to live according to the principles Jesus taught.

- Pursuing Righteousness: Seeking to live a life that reflects the character of Jesus.

The Parables of Jesus

Jesus often taught using parables, which convey deep spiritual truths through simple, relatable stories.

Matthew 13:44-46 (Parables of the Hidden Treasure and the Pearl):

"Again, the kingdom of heaven is like unto treasure hid in a field; the which when a man hath found, he hideth, and for joy thereof goeth and selleth all that he hath, and buyeth that field. Again, the kingdom of heaven is like unto a merchant man, seeking goodly pearls: Who, when he had found one pearl of great price, went and sold all that he had, and bought it."

Key Elements:

- Value of the Kingdom: These parables illustrate the incomparable value of the kingdom of heaven.

- Sacrificial Commitment: The willingness to give up everything for the sake of the kingdom.

Practical Applications:

- Valuing the Kingdom: Recognizing the supreme worth of God's kingdom and prioritizing it above all else.

- Commitment to God: Being willing to make sacrifices in our pursuit of God's kingdom.

The Miracles of Jesus

Jesus' miracles reveal His compassion, power, and authority over creation, sickness, and death.

Mark 4:39:

"And he arose, and rebuked the wind, and said unto the sea, Peace, be still. And the wind ceased, and there was a great calm."

Key Elements:

- Authority over Nature: Jesus' command over the natural elements demonstrates His divine authority.

John 11:43-44:

"And when he thus had spoken, he cried with a loud voice, Lazarus, come forth. And he that was dead came forth, bound hand and foot with graveclothes: and his face was bound about with a napkin. Jesus saith unto them, Loose him, and let him go."

Key Elements:

- Power Over Death: Jesus' raising of Lazarus from the dead underscores His power over life and death.

Practical Applications:

- Trusting in Jesus' Power: Believing in His ability to intervene in our lives miraculously.

- Seeking His Compassion: Approaching Jesus with our needs, knowing He is compassionate and powerful.

The Impact of Jesus' Sacrifice and Resurrection

Atonement for Sin

Jesus' sacrificial death on the cross provides atonement for sin, offering forgiveness and reconciliation with God.

Romans 5:8:

"But God commendeth his love toward us, in that, while we were yet sinners, Christ died for us."

Key Elements:

- Demonstration of Love: Jesus' death as the ultimate demonstration of God's love.

1 Peter 2:24:

"Who his own self bare our sins in his own body on the tree, that we, being dead to sins, should live unto righteousness: by whose stripes ye were healed."

Practical Applications:

- Receiving Forgiveness: Accepting Jesus' atonement and living in the freedom of forgiveness.

- Living Righteously: Responding to Jesus' sacrifice by pursuing a life of righteousness.

Victory Over Death

Jesus' resurrection signifies His victory over death, offering believers the hope of eternal life.

1 Corinthians 15:54-57:

"So when this corruptible shall have put on incorruption, and this mortal shall have put on immortality, then shall be brought to pass the saying that is written, Death is swallowed up in victory. O death, where is thy sting? O grave, where is thy victory? The sting of death is sin; and the strength of sin is the law. But thanks be to God, which giveth us the victory through our Lord Jesus Christ."

Key Elements:

- Victory Over Death: The resurrection as the ultimate triumph over death and sin.

- Hope of Eternal Life: Assurance of eternal life for believers.

Practical Applications:

- Living in Victory: Embracing the victory over death that Jesus has secured.

- Facing Life with Hope: Living with the confident expectation of eternal life.

Empowerment by the Holy Spirit

The resurrection and ascension of Jesus led to the outpouring of the Holy Spirit, empowering believers for life and ministry.

Acts 1:8:

"But ye shall receive power, after that the Holy Ghost is come upon you: and ye shall be witnesses unto me both in Jerusalem, and in all Judaea, and in Samaria, and unto the uttermost part of the earth."

Key Elements:

- Empowerment by the Holy Spirit: The indwelling presence of the Holy Spirit enabling believers to live out their faith.

Practical Applications:

- Living Spirit-Filled Lives: Relying on the Holy Spirit for guidance, strength, and transformation.

- Engaging in Mission: Being active witnesses of Jesus' resurrection and love.

Reflecting on the divinity and lessons of Jesus Christ offers believers a profound understanding of who He is and what He accomplished. Jesus, as the fulfillment of prophecy and the embodiment of God's love, invites us to live lives that reflect His teachings and the transformative power of His sacrifice and resurrection. His divine nature, illustrated through His miracles and teachings, and His victory over sin and death through His sacrifice and resurrection, provide a solid foundation for faith and hope.

As we continue to grow in our understanding and relationship with Jesus, let us embrace His teachings, live in the light of His sacrifice and resurrection, and be empowered by the Holy Spirit to share His love and truth with the world. Jesus Christ is not only the Savior of humanity but also the ultimate example of love, righteousness, and divine power, inviting us to follow Him and experience the fullness of life in Him.

CHAPTER 12

ENCOURAGEMENT TO LIVE ACCORDING TO HOS TEACHINGS

The teachings of Jesus Christ are not merely historical records or theological concepts but are living, transformative principles meant to guide our daily lives. His words challenge us to a higher standard of love, righteousness, and faithfulness. As followers of Christ, we are called to embody His teachings, allowing them to shape our character, decisions, and interactions with others. This chapter aims to provide encouragement and practical guidance for living according to the teachings of Jesus, emphasizing the profound impact this can have on our personal growth and witness to the world.

The Foundation of Jesus' Teachings

Love as the Greatest Commandment

Jesus emphasized love as the central commandment, summarizing the entire law and prophets.

Matthew 22:37-40:

"Jesus said unto him, Thou shalt love the Lord thy God with all thy heart, and with all thy soul, and with all thy mind. This is the first and great commandment. And the second is like unto it, Thou shalt love thy neighbour as thyself. On these two commandments hang all the law and the prophets."

Key Elements:

- Love for God: Complete devotion to God with our entire being.

- Love for Neighbor: Treating others with the same care and respect we desire for ourselves.

Practical Applications:

- Cultivating a Deep Relationship with God: Prioritizing prayer, worship, and Bible study to grow in our love for God.

- Practicing Active Compassion: Looking for opportunities to serve and show kindness to others.

The Call to Discipleship

Jesus calls His followers to a life of discipleship, marked by self-denial, taking up the cross, and following Him.

Matthew 16:24-25:

"Then said Jesus unto his disciples, If any man will come after me, let him deny himself, and take up his cross, and follow me. For whosoever will save his life shall lose it: and whosoever will lose his life for my sake shall find it."

Key Elements:

- Self-Denial: Putting aside our selfish desires to follow Christ.

- Taking Up the Cross: Willingness to endure hardship and sacrifice for Jesus' sake.

Practical Applications:

- Embracing Selflessness: Prioritizing the needs of others and the mission of Christ over our own comfort and desires.

- Enduring with Faith: Persevering through challenges and suffering with a focus on Jesus' example and promises.

Practical Steps to Live According to Jesus' Teachings

Developing a Christlike Character

The character of Jesus serves as a model for our own behavior and attitudes.

Galatians 5:22-23:

"But the fruit of the Spirit is love, joy, peace, longsuffering, gentleness, goodness, faith, Meekness, temperance: against such there is no law."

Key Elements:

- Fruit of the Spirit: Attributes that reflect the character of Christ.

Practical Applications:

- Cultivating Spiritual Fruit: Seeking the Holy Spirit's help to develop these attributes in our lives.

- Reflecting Christ's Character: Striving to exhibit love, joy, peace, patience, kindness, goodness, faithfulness, gentleness, and self-control in all we do.

Engaging in Active Service

Jesus demonstrated that greatness in His kingdom is found in serving others.

Mark 10:43-45:

"But so shall it not be among you: but whosoever will be great among you, shall be your minister: And whosoever of you will be the chiefest, shall be servant of all. For even the Son of man came not to be ministered unto, but to minister, and to give his life a ransom for many."

Key Elements:

- Servant Leadership: Leading by serving others, following Jesus' example.

Practical Applications:

- Serving with Humility: Looking for ways to serve others selflessly, both within the church and in the broader community.

- Empowering Others: Encouraging and supporting others in their gifts and callings.

Building Strong Relationships

Jesus emphasized the importance of loving relationships among His followers.

John 13:34-35:

"A new commandment I give unto you, That ye love one another; as I have loved you, that ye also love one another. By this shall all men know that ye are my disciples, if ye have love one to another."

Key Elements:

- Mutual Love: Loving one another as Jesus loves us.

- Witness of Unity: Demonstrating our discipleship through our love for one another.

Practical Applications:

- Fostering Community: Investing time and effort into building meaningful, supportive relationships with fellow believers.

- Practicing Forgiveness: Being quick to forgive and seek reconciliation when conflicts arise.

Overcoming Challenges in Living Out Jesus' Teachings

Dealing with Temptation

Jesus taught His disciples to be vigilant and prayerful to overcome temptation.

Matthew 26:41:

"Watch and pray, that ye enter not into temptation: the spirit indeed is willing, but the flesh is weak."

Key Elements:

- Vigilance in Prayer: Staying alert and prayerful to resist temptation.

Practical Applications:

- Maintaining Spiritual Discipline: Regularly engaging in prayer, Bible study, and fellowship to strengthen our spiritual resilience.

- Seeking Accountability: Finding trusted friends or mentors to provide support and accountability in areas of weakness.

Responding to Persecution

Jesus warned His followers that they would face persecution but encouraged them to remain steadfast.

John 15:18-20:

"If the world hate you, ye know that it hated me before it hated you. If ye were of the world, the world would love his own: but because ye are not of the world, but I have chosen you out of the world, therefore the world hateth you. Remember the word that I said unto you, The servant is not greater than his lord. If they have persecuted me, they will also persecute you; if they have kept my saying, they will keep yours also."

Key Elements:

- Endurance in Persecution: Remaining faithful despite opposition and suffering.

Practical Applications:

- Standing Firm in Faith: Holding onto our faith and convictions in the face of persecution.

- Praying for Persecutors: Following Jesus' example of praying for those who persecute us.

The Impact of Living According to Jesus' Teachings

Personal Transformation

Living according to Jesus' teachings leads to profound personal transformation, making us more like Him.

Romans 12:2:

"And be not conformed to this world: but be ye transformed by the renewing of your mind, that ye may prove what is that good, and acceptable, and perfect, will of God."

Key Elements:

- Renewal of the Mind: Allowing God's Word to transform our thinking and behavior.

Practical Applications:

- Daily Renewal: Regularly immersing ourselves in Scripture and allowing it to shape our thoughts and actions.

- Seeking God's Will: Aligning our lives with God's good, pleasing, and perfect will.

Witness to the World

Living out Jesus' teachings serves as a powerful witness to the world, drawing others to Him.

Matthew 5:14-16:

"Ye are the light of the world. A city that is set on an hill cannot be hid. Neither do men light a candle, and put it under a bushel, but on a candlestick; and it giveth light unto all that are in the house. Let your light so shine before men, that they may see your good works, and glorify your Father which is in heaven."

Key Elements:

- Light of the World: Our lives should shine with the light of Christ, illuminating the way for others.

Practical Applications:

- Living Authentically: Letting our faith be visible in all aspects of our lives.

- Engaging in Good Works: Actively seeking opportunities to do good and serve others, bringing glory to God.

Living according to the teachings of Jesus is a lifelong journey that transforms us and impacts those around us. His commands to love God and others, to serve selflessly, and to live righteously provide a clear roadmap for our lives. While challenges and temptations will arise, the Holy Spirit empowers us to remain faithful and steadfast.

As we strive to embody the teachings of Jesus, we experience personal transformation, strengthen our relationships, and become effective witnesses to the world. Let us be encouraged to continually seek Jesus, follow His example, and live in a way that reflects His love, grace, and truth, drawing others to the hope and salvation found in Him.

CHAPTER 13

FINAL THOUGHTS ON THE ENDURING RELEVANCE OF DANIEL'S PROPHECIES

The Book of Daniel stands as one of the most significant prophetic books in the Bible, providing profound insights into God's sovereignty, the rise and fall of empires, and the ultimate triumph of God's kingdom. Daniel's prophecies, written during a time of great turmoil and exile for the Israelites, continue to hold immense relevance for believers today. This chapter aims to reflect on the enduring relevance of Daniel's prophecies, examining their theological implications, their impact on our understanding of God's plan, and their practical applications for living a faithful life.

The Sovereignty of God

God's Control Over History

Daniel's prophecies underscore the sovereignty of God over the affairs of nations and the course of history.

Daniel 2:20-21:

"Daniel answered and said, Blessed be the name of God for ever and ever: for wisdom and might are his: And he changeth the times and the seasons: he removeth kings, and setteth up kings: he giveth wisdom unto the wise, and knowledge to them that know understanding."

Key Elements:

- Divine Sovereignty: God's authority over all earthly powers and events.

- Wisdom and Might: God's ultimate control and power to change the times and seasons.

Practical Applications:

- Trusting in God's Plan: Recognizing that God is in control, even amidst global turmoil and personal challenges.

- Seeking God's Wisdom: Turning to God for guidance and understanding in all circumstances.

The Rise and Fall of Kingdoms

Daniel's visions reveal the transient nature of earthly kingdoms and the eternal nature of God's kingdom.

Daniel 7:13-14:

"I saw in the night visions, and, behold, one like the Son of man came with the clouds of heaven, and came to the Ancient of days, and they brought him near before him. And there was given him dominion, and glory, and a kingdom, that all people, nations, and languages, should serve him: his dominion is an everlasting dominion, which shall not pass away, and his kingdom that which shall not be destroyed."

Key Elements:

- Everlasting Dominion: The eternal reign of the Son of Man, contrasted with the temporary nature of earthly powers.

- Universal Kingdom: A kingdom that encompasses all people, nations, and languages.

Practical Applications:

- Hope in God's Kingdom: Placing our hope in the enduring kingdom of God rather than in transient earthly powers.

- Living as Kingdom Citizens: Aligning our lives with the values and principles of God's eternal kingdom.

The Messiah in Daniel's Prophecies

The Anointed One

Daniel's prophecies point to the coming of the Messiah, who would bring redemption and establish God's kingdom.

Daniel 9:25-26:

"Know therefore and understand, that from the going forth of the commandment to restore and to build Jerusalem unto the Messiah the Prince shall be seven weeks, and threescore and two weeks: the street shall be built again, and the wall, even in troublous times. And after threescore and two weeks shall Messiah be cut off, but not for himself: and the people of the prince that shall come shall destroy the city and the sanctuary; and the end thereof shall be with a flood, and unto the end of the war desolations are determined."

Key Elements:

- Messiah the Prince: The anointed one who would come to bring salvation.

- Cut Off but Not for Himself: The sacrificial nature of the Messiah's mission.

Practical Applications:

- Recognizing Jesus as the Fulfillment: Seeing Jesus as the fulfillment of the Messianic prophecies in Daniel.

- Living in the Light of Redemption: Embracing the salvation that Jesus offers and living in gratitude for His sacrifice.

The Son of Man

Daniel's vision of the Son of Man has profound implications for understanding Jesus' role and identity.

Daniel 7:13-14:

"I saw in the night visions, and, behold, one like the Son of man came with the clouds of heaven, and came to the Ancient of days, and they brought him near before him. And there was given him dominion, and glory, and a kingdom, that all people, nations, and languages, should serve him: his dominion is an everlasting dominion, which shall not pass away, and his kingdom that which shall not be destroyed."

Key Elements:

- Son of Man: A Messianic title that Jesus frequently used to describe Himself.

- Eternal Kingdom: The everlasting reign of the Messiah.

Practical Applications:

- Worshiping Jesus as King: Acknowledging Jesus' authority and submitting to His lordship.

- Spreading the Good News: Sharing the message of Jesus' eternal kingdom with others.

The End Times and Eternal Hope

Prophecies of the End Times

Daniel provides a glimpse into the end times, offering hope and assurance of God's ultimate victory.

Daniel 12:1-3:

"And at that time shall Michael stand up, the great prince which standeth for the children of thy people: and there shall be a time of trouble, such as never was since there was a nation even to that same time: and at that time thy people shall be delivered, every one that shall be found written in the book. And many of them that sleep in the dust of the earth shall awake, some to everlasting life, and some to shame and everlasting contempt. And they that be wise shall shine as the brightness of the firmament; and they that turn many to righteousness as the stars forever and ever."

Key Elements:

- Time of Trouble: A period of great tribulation preceding the end.

- Resurrection and Judgment: The resurrection of the dead and the final judgment.

- Eternal Rewards: The promise of everlasting life and glory for the righteous.

Practical Applications:

- Preparing for the End Times: Living with an awareness of the coming judgment and striving to remain faithful.

- Encouraging Righteousness: Leading others to righteousness and faith in Jesus.

Eternal Perspective

Daniel's prophecies encourage believers to maintain an eternal perspective, focusing on God's ultimate plan rather than temporary struggles.

2 Corinthians 4:17-18:

"For our light affliction, which is but for a moment, worketh for us a far more exceeding and eternal weight of glory; While we look not at the things which are seen, but at the things which are not seen: for the things which are seen are temporal; but the things which are not seen are eternal."

Key Elements:

- Eternal Weight of Glory: The incomparable value of eternal rewards.

- Temporal vs. Eternal: Distinguishing between temporary struggles and eternal truths.

Practical Applications:

- Focusing on Eternity: Keeping our eyes fixed on eternal promises rather than temporary difficulties.

- Persevering in Faith: Enduring hardships with the hope of eternal glory.

Living in Response to Daniel's Prophecies

Faithfulness in Adversity

Daniel's life exemplifies faithfulness in the face of adversity, providing a model for believers today.

Daniel 6:10:

"Now when Daniel knew that the writing was signed, he went into his house; and his windows being open in his chamber toward Jerusalem, he kneeled upon his knees three times a day, and prayed, and gave thanks before his God, as he did aforetime."

Key Elements:

- Consistency in Prayer: Daniel's unwavering commitment to prayer and worship.

- Courage in Persecution: Daniel's boldness in maintaining his faith despite the threat of persecution.

Practical Applications:

- Maintaining Spiritual Disciplines: Committing to regular prayer, worship, and study of God's Word.

- Standing Firm in Faith: Being courageous and steadfast in our faith, regardless of external pressures.

Wisdom and Understanding

Daniel was renowned for his wisdom and understanding, gifts that God bestowed upon him and that can guide us today.

Daniel 1:17:

"As for these four children, God gave them knowledge and skill in all learning and wisdom: and Daniel had understanding in all visions and dreams."

Key Elements:

- Divine Wisdom: The wisdom and understanding that come from God.

- Application of Knowledge: Using God-given wisdom to navigate life's challenges.

Practical Applications:

- Seeking God's Wisdom: Praying for and pursuing wisdom and understanding in all areas of life.

- Applying Biblical Principles: Utilizing the knowledge and insights from Scripture to make wise decisions.

The prophecies of Daniel remain profoundly relevant for believers today. They remind us of God's sovereignty over history, the assured victory of His kingdom, and the hope of resurrection and eternal life. Daniel's example of faithfulness, wisdom, and courage in adversity serves as a powerful model for living a life that honors God.

As we reflect on Daniel's prophecies, let us be encouraged to trust in God's plan, live with an eternal perspective, and faithfully follow Jesus, the fulfillment of these ancient prophecies. By doing so, we can navigate the challenges of our time with hope and confidence, knowing that we are part of God's unshakable kingdom.

APPENDIX A

CHRONOLOGICAL OF DANIEL'S PROPHECIES AND THEIR FULFILLMENT

The Book of Daniel contains some of the most detailed and significant prophecies in the Bible, spanning from Daniel's own time in the 6th century BCE to the end times. Understanding the chronology of these prophecies and their fulfillment is crucial for appreciating the scope and accuracy of biblical prophecy. This appendix provides a chronological overview of Daniel's prophecies and their fulfillment, offering a timeline that highlights key events and their significance.

Prophecies During Daniel's Time

The Dream of Nebuchadnezzar (Daniel 2)

Date: Approximately 603-602 BCE

Prophecy: King Nebuchadnezzar's dream of a great statue composed of different materials, each representing successive kingdoms.

Daniel 2:31-35:

"Thou, O king, sawest, and behold a great image. This great image, whose brightness was excellent, stood before thee; and the form thereof was terrible. This image's head was of fine gold, his breast and his arms of silver, his belly and his thighs of brass, His legs of iron, his feet part of iron and part of clay. Thou sawest till that a stone was cut out without hands, which smote the image upon his feet that were of iron and clay, and brake them to pieces."

Fulfillment:

- Head of Gold: Babylonian Empire (626-539 BCE)

- Chest and Arms of Silver: Medo-Persian Empire (539-331 BCE)

- Belly and Thighs of Bronze: Greek Empire (331-146 BCE)

- Legs of Iron and Feet of Iron and Clay: Roman Empire (146 BCE-476 CE)

- Stone Cut Without Hands: The establishment of God's eternal kingdom through Jesus Christ.

The Vision of the Four Beasts (Daniel 7)

Date: Approximately 553 BCE

Prophecy: Daniel's vision of four great beasts rising from the sea, each symbolizing different empires.

Daniel 7:3-7:

"And four great beasts came up from the sea, diverse one from another. The first was like a lion, and had eagle's wings: I beheld till the wings thereof were plucked, and it was lifted up from the earth, and made stand upon the feet as a man, and a man's heart was given to it. And behold another beast, a second, like to a bear, and it raised up itself on one side, and it had three ribs in the mouth of it between the teeth of it: and they said thus unto it, Arise, devour much flesh. After this I beheld, and lo another, like a leopard, which had upon the back of it four wings of a fowl; the beast had also four heads; and dominion was given to it. After this I saw in the night visions, and behold a fourth beast, dreadful and terrible, and strong exceedingly; and it had great iron teeth: it devoured and brake in pieces, and stamped the residue with the feet of it: and it was diverse from all the beasts that were before it; and it had ten horns."

Fulfillment:

- Lion with Eagle's Wings: Babylonian Empire

- Bear: Medo-Persian Empire

- Leopard with Four Wings: Greek Empire

- Terrible Beast with Ten Horns: Roman Empire and its eventual division.

Prophecies of the Future

The Vision of the Ram and Goat (Daniel 8)

Date: Approximately 551 BCE

Prophecy: Daniel's vision of a ram with two horns and a goat with a prominent horn, which breaks the ram's horns.

Daniel 8:3-7:

"Then I lifted up mine eyes, and saw, and, behold, there stood before the river a ram which had two horns: and the two horns were high; but one was higher than the other, and the higher came up last. I saw the ram pushing westward, and northward, and southward; so that no beasts might stand before him, neither was there any that could deliver out of his hand; but he did according to his will, and became great. And as I was considering, behold, an he goat came from the west on the face of the whole earth, and touched not the ground: and the goat had a notable horn between his eyes. And he came to the ram that had two horns, which I had seen standing before the river, and ran unto him in the fury of his power."

Fulfillment:

- Ram with Two Horns: Medo-Persian Empire

- Goat with a Prominent Horn: Greek Empire under Alexander the Great

- Breaking of the Ram's Horns: The defeat of the Medo-Persian Empire by Alexander the Great in 331 BCE.

The Seventy Weeks Prophecy (Daniel 9:24-27)

Date: Approximately 538 BCE

Prophecy: Daniel's vision of seventy weeks (490 years) outlining the timeline for the coming of the Messiah and the end of sin.

Daniel 9:24-27:

"Seventy weeks are determined upon thy people and upon thy holy city, to finish the transgression, and to make an end of sins, and to make reconciliation for iniquity, and to bring in everlasting righteousness, and to seal up the vision and prophecy, and to anoint the most Holy. Know therefore and understand, that from the going forth of the commandment to restore and to build Jerusalem unto the Messiah the Prince shall be seven weeks, and threescore and two weeks: the street shall be built again, and the wall, even in troublous times. And after threescore and two weeks shall Messiah be cut off, but not for himself: and the people of the prince that shall come shall destroy the city and the sanctuary; and the end thereof shall be with a flood, and unto the end of the war desolations are determined. And he shall confirm the

covenant with many for one week: and in the midst of the week he shall cause the sacrifice and the oblation to cease, and for the overspreading of abominations he shall make it desolate, even until the consummation, and that determined shall be poured upon the desolate."

Fulfillment:

- Command to Restore Jerusalem: Issued by Artaxerxes I in 445 BCE (Nehemiah 2:1-8)

- Seven Weeks and Sixty-Two Weeks: 69 weeks (483 years) from 445 BCE to the arrival of Jesus as the Messiah.

- Messiah Cut Off: The crucifixion of Jesus around 30-33 CE.

- Destruction of Jerusalem: Fulfilled in 70 CE when the Romans destroyed Jerusalem and the temple.

The Time of the End (Daniel 12)

Date: Approximately 535 BCE

Prophecy: Daniel's vision of the end times, including the resurrection of the dead and the final judgment.

Daniel 12:1-3:

"And at that time shall Michael stand up, the great prince which standeth for the children of thy people: and there shall be a time of trouble, such as never was since there was a nation even to that same time: and at that time thy people shall be delivered, every one that shall be found written in the book. And many of them that sleep in the dust of the earth shall awake, some to everlasting life, and some to shame and everlasting contempt. And they that be wise shall shine as the brightness of the firmament; and they that turn many to righteousness as the stars for ever and ever."

Fulfillment:

- Time of Trouble: Often associated with the Great Tribulation described in the New Testament (Matthew 24:21).

- Resurrection of the Dead: Future event linked to the second coming of Christ and the final judgment (1 Thessalonians 4:16-17; Revelation 20:11-15).

The chronology of Daniel's prophecies demonstrates the precision and reliability of biblical prophecy. From the rise and fall of ancient empires to the coming of the Messiah and the ultimate victory of God's kingdom, Daniel's visions provide a comprehensive overview of God's redemptive plan for humanity. These prophecies not only validate the divine inspiration of Scripture but also offer believers hope and assurance in God's sovereign control over history.

By understanding the chronology of Daniel's prophecies and their fulfillment, we can deepen our faith, gain a greater appreciation for God's plan, and live with the confidence that His promises will be fulfilled. As we reflect on these prophecies, let us be encouraged to trust in God's sovereignty, remain faithful in our walk with Him, and look forward to the ultimate fulfillment of His kingdom.

KEY BIBLE VERSES AND THEIR EXPLANATION

The Book of Daniel is rich with prophetic visions and profound insights into God's sovereignty, the rise and fall of kingdoms, and the coming of the Messiah. This appendix provides key Bible verses from Daniel along with explanations to help readers understand their significance and relevance.

Key Verses and Explanations

Daniel 2:20-21

Verse:

"Daniel answered and said, Blessed be the name of God for ever and ever: for wisdom and might are his: And he changeth the times and the seasons: he removeth kings, and setteth up kings: he giveth wisdom unto the wise, and knowledge to them that know understanding."

Explanation:

These verses highlight God's sovereignty over history and His control over the rise and fall of leaders and nations. Daniel praises God for His wisdom and power, acknowledging that all changes in political and natural orders are under God's authority. This acknowledgment serves as a reminder of God's ultimate control and the temporary nature of earthly powers.

Daniel 2:44

Verse:

"And in the days of these kings shall the God of heaven set up a kingdom, which shall never be destroyed: and the kingdom shall not be left to other people, but it shall break in pieces and consume all these kingdoms, and it shall stand for ever."

Explanation:

This verse prophesies the establishment of God's eternal kingdom, which will surpass and outlast all earthly kingdoms. It emphasizes the final victory and enduring nature of God's reign, providing hope and assurance to believers of God's ultimate plan for history.

Daniel 7:13-14

Verse:

"I saw in the night visions, and, behold, one like the Son of man came with the clouds of heaven, and came to the Ancient of days, and they brought him near before him. And there was given him dominion, and glory, and a kingdom, that all people, nations, and languages, should serve him: his dominion is an everlasting dominion, which shall not pass away, and his kingdom that which shall not be destroyed."

Explanation:

This vision of the "Son of man" coming with the clouds of heaven is a key Messianic prophecy. It signifies the coming of Jesus Christ, who frequently referred to Himself as the "Son of Man." The passage emphasizes the universal and eternal dominion of Christ's kingdom, highlighting the fulfillment of God's redemptive plan through Jesus.

Daniel 9:24-27

Verse:

"Seventy weeks are determined upon thy people and upon thy holy city, to finish the transgression, and to make an end of sins, and to make reconciliation for iniquity, and to bring in everlasting righteousness, and to seal up the vision and prophecy, and to anoint the most Holy. Know therefore and understand, that from the going forth of the commandment to restore and to build Jerusalem unto the

Messiah the Prince shall be seven weeks, and threescore and two weeks: the street shall be built again, and the wall, even in troublous times. And after threescore and two weeks shall Messiah be cut off, but not for himself: and the people of the prince that shall come shall destroy the city and the sanctuary; and the end thereof shall be with a flood, and unto the end of the war desolations are determined. And he shall confirm the covenant with many for one week: and in the midst of the week he shall cause the sacrifice and the oblation to cease, and for the overspreading of abominations he shall make it desolate, even until the consummation, and that determined shall be poured upon the desolate."

Explanation:

This passage, known as the Seventy Weeks Prophecy, outlines a timeline for the coming of the Messiah and the events leading to the end times. It predicts the arrival of Jesus Christ, His sacrificial death, and the eventual destruction of Jerusalem. The prophecy highlights God's plan for redemption and judgment, emphasizing the significance of Jesus' atoning work.

Daniel 12:1-3

Verse:

"And at that time shall Michael stand up, the great prince which standeth for the children of thy people: and there shall be a time of trouble, such as never was since there was a nation even to that same time: and at that time thy people shall be delivered, every one that shall be found written in the book. And many of them that sleep in the dust of the earth shall awake, some to everlasting life, and some to shame and everlasting contempt. And they that be wise shall shine as the brightness of the firmament; and they that turn many to righteousness as the stars for ever and ever."

Explanation:

These verses describe the end times, including a period of great tribulation, the resurrection of the dead, and the final judgment. The passage provides hope for believers, assuring them of deliverance and eternal life. It also underscores the importance of wisdom and leading others to righteousness, highlighting the eternal rewards for the faithful.

The key verses from the Book of Daniel offer profound insights into God's sovereignty, the coming of the Messiah, and the ultimate triumph of His kingdom. Understanding these verses helps believers appreciate the continuity of God's redemptive plan and the assurance of His eternal reign. By reflecting on these prophecies and their fulfillment, we can deepen our faith and live with the confident hope that God's promises will be fulfilled.

APPENDIX C

REFERENCES AND FURTHER READING

For those who wish to delve deeper into the Book of Daniel, its prophecies, and their fulfillment, numerous scholarly works and theological resources provide valuable insights and comprehensive analyses. This appendix lists key references and further reading materials that can enhance understanding and appreciation of Daniel's prophecies and their significance.

Key References

1. The Holy Bible

- Translations: King James Version (KJV), New International Version (NIV), English Standard Version (ESV), New American Standard Bible (NASB)

- Study Bibles: The ESV Study Bible, The NIV Study Bible, The MacArthur Study Bible

2. Commentaries on Daniel

- Baldwin, Joyce G. "Daniel: An Introduction and Commentary". Tyndale Old Testament Commentaries. InterVarsity Press, 1978.

- Collins, John J. "Daniel: A Commentary on the Book of Daniel". Hermeneia: A Critical and Historical Commentary on the Bible. Fortress Press, 1993.

- Goldingay, John E. "Daniel". Word Biblical Commentary, Vol. 30. Zondervan, 1989.

- Miller, Stephen R. "Daniel". The New American Commentary, Vol. 18. B&H Publishing Group, 1994.

- Longman, Tremper III. "Daniel". The NIV Application Commentary. Zondervan, 1999.

3. Books on Biblical Prophecy

- Archer, Gleason L. "The Expositor's Bible Commentary, Volume 7: Daniel and the Minor Prophets". Zondervan, 1986.

- Walvoord, John F. "Daniel: The Key to Prophetic Revelation". Moody Publishers, 1971.

- Young, Edward J. "The Prophecy of Daniel: A Commentary". Eerdmans, 1949.

- LaHaye, Tim, and Thomas Ice. "Charting the End Times: A Visual Guide to Understanding Bible Prophecy". Harvest House Publishers, 2001.

4. Theological Dictionaries and Encyclopedias

- Bromiley, Geoffrey W. "The International Standard Bible Encyclopedia". Eerdmans, 1979-1988.

- Freedman, David Noel, ed. "The Anchor Bible Dictionary". Doubleday, 1992.

- Tenney, Merrill C., and Moisés Silva, eds. "The Zondervan Encyclopedia of the Bible". Zondervan, 2009.

5. Historical Context and Background Studies

- Bright, John. "A History of Israel". Westminster John Knox Press, 2000.

- Kitchen, K.A. "On the Reliability of the Old Testament". Eerdmans, 2003.

- Wiseman, Donald J. "Chronicles of Chaldaean Kings (626-556 B.C.) in the British Museum". Trustees of the British Museum, 1956.

Further Reading

1. Studies on Daniel's Prophecies

- Ford, Desmond. "Daniel". Southern Publishing Association, 1978.

- Goldsworthy, Graeme. "The Son of Man and the Saints of the Most High in the Book of Daniel". Journal of Biblical Literature, 93.1, 1974.

2. Apocalyptic Literature

- Collins, John J. "The Apocalyptic Imagination: An Introduction to Jewish Apocalyptic Literature". Eerdmans, 1998.

- Hanson, Paul D. "The Dawn of Apocalyptic". Fortress Press, 1979.

3. Messianic Prophecies

- Kaiser, Walter C. Jr. "The Messiah in the Old Testament". Zondervan, 1995.

- Pate, C. Marvin. "70 Weeks Are Determined: The Historical and Prophetic Fulfillment of Daniel 9". Prophecy Watchers, 2020.

4. Biblical Theology

- Beale, G.K. "A New Testament Biblical Theology: The Unfolding of the Old Testament in the New". Baker Academic, 2011.

- Carson, D.A., and G.K. Beale, eds. "Commentary on the New Testament Use of the Old Testament". Baker Academic, 2007.

Online Resources

1. Bible Study Tools

- Blue Letter Bible (www.blueletterbible.org)

- Bible Gateway (www.biblegateway.com)

- Crosswalk (www.crosswalk.com)

2. Scholarly Articles and Journals

- Journal of Biblical Literature (www.sbl-site.org/publications/journals_jbl.aspx)

- Theological Studies (www.theologicalstudies.org.uk)

- Biblical Archaeology Review (www.biblicalarchaeology.org)

3. Lectures and Sermons

- The Gospel Coalition (www.thegospelcoalition.org)

- Desiring God (www.desiringgod.org)

- Ligonier Ministries (www.ligonier.org)

The study of Daniel's prophecies offers profound insights into God's sovereignty, the unfolding of redemptive history, and the hope of Christ's eternal kingdom. By engaging with the resources and further reading materials listed in this appendix, readers can deepen their understanding of biblical prophecy and its enduring relevance. These works provide comprehensive analyses, historical context, and theological reflections that enrich the study of the Book of Daniel and its significance for believers today.

BIBLIOGRAPHY

Primary Sources

1. The Holy Bible

- King James Version (KJV)

- New International Version (NIV)

- English Standard Version (ESV)

- New American Standard Bible (NASB)

Commentaries on Daniel

2. Baldwin, Joyce G. "Daniel: An Introduction and Commentary." Tyndale Old Testament Commentaries. InterVarsity Press, 1978.

3. Collins, John J. "Daniel: A Commentary on the Book of Daniel." Hermeneia: A Critical and Historical Commentary on the Bible. Fortress Press, 1993.

4. Goldingay, John E. "Daniel." Word Biblical Commentary, Vol. 30. Zondervan, 1989.

5. Miller, Stephen R. "Daniel." The New American Commentary, Vol. 18. B&H Publishing Group, 1994.

6. Longman, Tremper III. "Daniel." The NIV Application Commentary. Zondervan, 1999.

Books on Biblical Prophecy

7. Archer, Gleason L. "The Expositor's Bible Commentary, Volume 7: Daniel and the Minor Prophets." Zondervan, 1986.

8. Walvoord, John F. "Daniel: The Key to Prophetic Revelation." Moody Publishers, 1971.

9. Young, Edward J. "The Prophecy of Daniel: A Commentary." Eerdmans, 1949.

10. LaHaye, Tim, and Thomas Ice. "Charting the End Times: A Visual Guide to Understanding Bible Prophecy." Harvest House Publishers, 2001.

Theological Dictionaries and Encyclopedias

11. Bromiley, Geoffrey W. "The International Standard Bible Encyclopedia." Eerdmans, 1979-1988.

12. Freedman, David Noel, ed. "The Anchor Bible Dictionary." Doubleday, 1992.

13. Tenney, Merrill C., and Moisés Silva, eds. "The Zondervan Encyclopedia of the Bible." Zondervan, 2009.

Historical Context and Background Studies

14. Bright, John. "A History of Israel." Westminster John Knox Press, 2000.

15. Kitchen, K.A. "On the Reliability of the Old Testament." Eerdmans, 2003.

16. Wiseman, Donald J. "Chronicles of Chaldaean Kings (626-556 B.C.) in the British Museum." Trustees of the British Museum, 1956.

Further Reading on Daniel's Prophecies

17. Ford, Desmond. "Daniel." Southern Publishing Association, 1978.

18. Goldsworthy, Graeme. "The Son of Man and the Saints of the Most High in the Book of Daniel." Journal of Biblical Literature, 93.1, 1974.

Apocalyptic Literature

19. Collins, John J. "The Apocalyptic Imagination: An Introduction to Jewish Apocalyptic Literature." Eerdmans, 1998.

20. Hanson, Paul D. "The Dawn of Apocalyptic." Fortress Press, 1979.

Messianic Prophecies

21. Kaiser, Walter C. Jr. "The Messiah in the Old Testament." Zondervan, 1995.

22. Pate, C. Marvin. "70 Weeks Are Determined: The Historical and Prophetic Fulfillment of Daniel 9." Prophecy Watchers, 2020.

Biblical Theology

23. Beale, G.K. "A New Testament Biblical Theology: The Unfolding of the Old Testament in the New." Baker Academic, 2011.

24. Carson, D.A., and G.K. Beale, eds. "Commentary on the New Testament Use of the Old Testament." Baker Academic, 2007.

Online Resources

25. Blue Letter Bible (www.blueletterbible.org)

26. Bible Gateway (www.biblegateway.com)

27. Crosswalk (www.crosswalk.com)

Scholarly Articles and Journals

28. Journal of Biblical Literature (www.sbl-site.org/publications/journals_jbl.aspx)

29. Theological Studies (www.theologicalstudies.org.uk)

30. Biblical Archaeology Review (www.biblicalarchaeology.org)

Lectures and Sermons

31. The Gospel Coalition (www.thegospelcoalition.org)

32. Desiring God (www.desiringgod.org)

33. Ligonier Ministries (www.ligonier.org)

This bibliography lists the primary sources and scholarly works referenced throughout the book. These resources provide a comprehensive foundation for the study of the Book of Daniel and its prophetic significance. They include biblical texts, commentaries, theological dictionaries, historical studies, and further reading materials to enhance understanding and provide deeper insights into the themes and prophecies of Daniel.